About Island Press

Island Press, a nonprofit organization, publishes, markets, and distributes the most advanced thinking on the conservation of our natural resources—books about soil, land, water, forests, wildlife, and hazardous and toxic wastes. These books are practical tools used by public officials, business and industry leaders, natural resource managers, and concerned citizens working to solve both local and global resource problems.

Founded in 1978, Island Press reorganized in 1984 to meet the increasing demand for substantive books on all resource-related issues. Island Press publishes and distributes under its own imprint and offers these services to other nonprofit organizations.

Funding to support Island Press is provided by Apple Computers, Inc., The Mary Reynolds Babcock Foundation, The Educational Foundation of America, The Charles Engelhard Foundation, The Ford Foundation, The George Gund Foundation, The William and Flora Hewlett Foundation, The Joyce Foundation, The J. M. Kaplan Fund, The John D. and Catherine T. MacArthur Foundation, The Andrew W. Mellon Foundation, The Joyce Mertz-Gilmore Foundation, The New-Land Foundation, Northwest Area Foundation, The Jessie Smith Noyes Foundation, The J. N. Pew, Jr., Charitable Trust, The Rockefeller Brothers Fund, The Florence and John Schumann Foundation, The Tides Foundation, and individual donors.

Overtapped Oasis

Overtapped

Oasis

Reform or Revolution for Western Water

Marc Reisner and Sarah Bates

Foreword by Bruce Babbitt

ISLAND PRESS

Washington, D.C. □ Covelo, California

Photograph by Baron Wolman

The authors are grateful for permission to include the following previously copyrighted material:
The map on page 9 was reprinted from *Groundwater Contamination in the United States,* by Veronica I. Pye, Ruth Patrick, and John Quarles. Philadelphia: University of Pennsylyania Press, 1983.
The maps on pages 36 and 39 were reprinted, with permission, from *Scarce Water and Institutional Change,* Kenneth D. Frederick, ed., with the assistance of Diana C. Gibbons. Copyright 1986 Resources for the Future, Washington, D.C.

Library of Congress Cataloging-in-Publication Data

Reisner, Marc.
    Overtapped oasis : reform or revolution for western water / Marc Reisner and Sarah Bates ; foreword by Bruce Babbitt.
        p. cm.
    ISBN 0-933280-76-9 (alk. paper)
    1. 0933280750 (pbk. : alk. paper)   2. Water-supply—Government policy—West (U.S.)   3. Water resources development—Government policy—West (U.S.)   4. Water conservation—Government policy—West (U.S.)   I. Bates, Sarah, 1962–   . II. Title.
HD1695.A17R45   1990
333.91'00978—dc20   89-24459
                                                                                    CIP

Contents ▉▉▉▉▉▉▉▉〰〰〰

Contents

Contents

Foreword

Once or twice a year I go to the Grand Canyon in search of solitude and perspective. On my last trip I hiked down from the North Rim to Nankoweap Basin, camped by the river, did a little fishing, and waited for a passing boat to take me downstream. Even on that beach, right in the middle of the greatest national park on the planet, the Bureau of Reclamation has managed to slip in and rearrange the scenery. A hundred miles upstream at Glen Canyon Dam, the bureau runs the electric generators to squeeze out the last dollar to subsidize ever more reclamation projects. As a result, the river by my campsite cycled up and down as the faucet at Glen Canyon was turned on and off. In the afternoon the river was low, and great bars of wet rock, covered with moss and slime, stood above the river. In the morning the river ran high, the rock bars were gone, and the beach beneath my sleeping bag was cracked and caving into the water.

In *Cadillac Desert* Marc Reisner took us for an entertaining ride through western history, beginning in the days when dam builders worked with people to bring water to the land and open the West to settlement. He showed us how engineers and promoters went on to turn the Bureau of Reclamation into a political machine that couldn't stop and finally became a parody of itself.

In this book Reisner is back, with Sarah Bates, to talk about the future. Whether we like it or not, the West doesn't have enough water for everyone to do everything, and because of economic and environmental reasons, we are beyond the days of calling in the Bureau of Reclamation to rescue us by building more dams.

Reisner and Bates don't suggest that the West has no future. Quite the contrary. They tell us that by putting economics back into the water equation there is still plenty of water available for those users willing to pay the real price. In other words, agriculture, which uses 85 percent of the water in the West, must yield some of its water to be reallocated to growing cities and urban areas and protecting wilderness and wildlife. This process is called *water marketing,* and it is beginning to happen throughout the West. But, say Reisner and Bates, the transition could take place more smoothly and equitably if we would only reform the outdated legal institutions that keep water tied to the land and prevent transfers, even when a willing farmer is ready to sell to a willing city. They are right, and they have good recommendations for reform.

BRUCE BABBITT
Former Governor of Arizona

Preface

Ten years ago, in 1979, I was just starting to work on a history of water and the American West entitled *Cadillac Desert*. When I began research for the book, Jimmy Carter's one-term presidency was stumbling to a close. Commentators have blamed his single term of office on America's humiliation in Iran, on the oil shortage of 1978 and 1979, on inflation, and on Carter's quirky style, but in my view his demise can be traced all the way back to 1977. It was in that year, just a few weeks after he became president, that Carter floated his "hit list" of already authorized water projects which he did not want built. Much of what a president does early in his term is forgotten or forgiven, even by those who strenuously disagree with him, but Carter's antipathy toward water projects, and his ineffectual effort to take an axe to the congressional pork barrel, were to haunt him for the rest of his term. Many members of Congress, and most westerners, regarded the hit list as a virtual declaration of war, and Carter's fondness for wild, untamed rivers was viewed by some of them as "just plain kooky." (The phrase was offered by one of Carter's top advisers, who may have felt that way himself.)

Watching Carter blown over backwards by the reaction, it seemed to me that the West's, and Congress's, infatuation with water projects would never end. So *Cadillac Desert* was conceived as a work of history with a warning attached—that earlier desert civilizations had overreached themselves in their passion to make the desert flower and had come to grief. Through salted-out land or silted-up dams or some other expensive, unforeseen reckoning, nature had exacted a grim retribution. It was a message, I thought, that few Americans had heard above the din of the earthmovers and Caterpillars erecting monumental dams in the river canyons of the American West.

I was probably right in 1979 when I started out, but by 1986, when the book was published, I began to wonder. One reviewer said the message was as dated as "a passionate appeal ... for women's right to vote." It is not my habit to agree with critical reviews, but there was a *little* something to that. In the seven years it took me to write *Cadillac Desert*, the water development juggernaut that had rolled relentlessly forward since the Great Depression ground pretty much to a halt. Between 1902 and 1930, the federal government built about fifty dams. Between 1930 and 1980, it built a thousand more. Since 1980, it has built virtually none. Ronald Reagan proved as uninterested in more water development as Carter was opposed to it, and Reagan in fact achieved much of what Carter had only sought. Former Colorado Governor Richard Lamm, one of many self-anointed environmentalists who fought Carter truculently over the hit list, has now come to the conclusion that Colorado's water is much more valuable left in its rivers than diverted to irrigated alfalfa fields. Huge dams whose construction seemed inevitable a few years ago—Auburn in California, Two Forks in Colorado, Orme in Arizona, O'Neill in Nebraska—now look as if they will never be built. Even the Bureau of Reclamation has been forced to concede that the Dam Era is over—or, perhaps, it may secretly hope, over for now.

The great issue is what will take its place. The rate of population growth in the West has not slowed at all in the past twenty years; since 1978, California has added the population of Missouri, Mississippi, and Maine. Groundwater is still overdrafted recklessly; in California and on the High Plains alone, underground water is being mined at a rate of 5 trillion gallons a year. Without vastly greater efficiency or a redistribution of the available water, America's desert empire will become more and more vulnerable in the years ahead. But how do you achieve redistribution without creating ghost acreage and ghost towns and destroying the economy and culture of the rural, essential West? Without fostering chaotic, explosive, and perhaps unsustainable development in its desert cities?

When Jim Butcher, then of the Rural Poverty and Resources Division at the Ford Foundation, called me up early in 1987 and invited me to write a "sequel" to *Cadillac Desert*, an inquiry of that nature was not what he had in mind. His focus was more narrow: How easily might the West survive the interment of its godfather for water development—the U.S. Bureau of Reclamation? That question seemed interesting enough to me. So I accepted his invitation, began to proceed, and was immediately in over my head. I knew that the doctrine of western water law and the policies it has spawned are complex and perverse; I had not appreciated how much so. If you simply abolished the bureau, little would change under the status quo except that cities, states, and irrigation districts would end up building more of their own dams. Water would continue to be inefficiently used, as would the diversion of whole rivers for what rational people might deem irrational purposes. Meanwhile, under existing law and policy, growing cities would in many cases be prohibited from buying water from farmers whose fields are nearly drowned. And the natural environment would be ever more deprived of the liquid nourishment it so desperately needs.

It was soon obvious that, once and for all, I was going to have to make myself understand water law. And since most important water policy is set at the state level, I was going to have to analyze the sometimes strikingly different codes of the various states and, in some cases, suggest wholesale revisions. I was going to have to think of strategies for returning water to the natural environment that made at least some legal sense.

What I needed, in other words, was a lawyer—a lawyer who had not only made a specialty of water law but who had great energy and a capacity for original thinking. It was my good fortune to find such a rare blend of attributes in the person of

Sarah Bates, who had just graduated from the University of Colorado School of Law, where she was closely affiliated with its Natural Resources Law Center. Sarah's contributions to the manuscript were so considerable that it would have done her an injustice to call her anything less than coauthor.

Thanks also to David Getches of the University of Colorado School of Law, a nationally recognized authority on water and law who agreed to be a member of our advisory committee and helped shepherd along the project from the beginning. Other members were Guy Martin, who served as assistant interior secretary for land and water in the Carter administration; Richard Howitt, who teaches agricultural economics at the University of California at Davis; Jan van Schilfgaarde, formerly director of the Department of Agriculture's Salinity Control Laboratory and now assistant director of the Agricultural Research Service, Northern Plains Region; Luna Leopold, former director of the U.S. Geological Survey and an eminent geohydrologist (his father's spirit guided us throughout the course of writing this book); and Bruce Driver, a lawyer and water expert affiliated with the Western Governors' Association. The members of the advisory committee kept us as factual, honest, and consistent as they could; they have our thanks. Any errors the reader may find are ours, not theirs.

I would also like to acknowledge the help of Steven Shupe, who offered constructive criticism without being obliged to; Jan Cornwell, who typed innumerable revisions and survived; and Don Yoder, for his thorough copyediting. I must also express much appreciation to Jim Butcher, Dr. Norman Collins, the Ford Foundation, which funded the entire project, and to Island Press, a true conscience of the publishing industry.

MARC REISNER

Overtapped Oasis

Introduction ▬▬▬▬▬▬▬▬▬▬

It has been just one hundred twenty years since John Wesley Powell rode through the canyons of the Colorado River in a wooden dory. In that brief period—an eyeblink if your clock is set to geological time—a good piece of the American West has become an unrecognizably altered place. Powell's exploration of the last uncharted quarter of the United States signified, as well as anything could, the closing of the frontier, and no frontier ever came to such an abrupt end. In 1869, when Powell pushed his boats onto Utah's Green River, the population of greater Los Angeles was barely 13,000; now the basin holds 13 million. California's Great Central Valley still had grizzly bears, antelope, and tens of millions of migratory waterfowl; today, it is a seamless, wall-to-wall carpet of agricultural crops. What is now central Arizona had fewer inhabitants per square mile than parts of the Sahara Desert; today, it is one of the most densely populated true deserts in the world. The plains below Colorado's Front Range were a sea of grazing buffalo and antelope when Powell was a young man; a checkerboard of crops when he was an old man; today, a sprawl of tract homes.

3

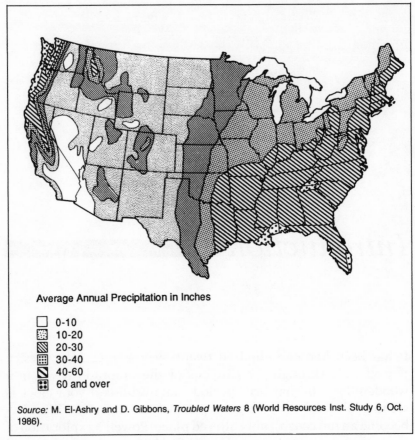

Average Annual Precipitation in Inches

☐ 0-10
▨ 10-20
▧ 20-30
▦ 30-40
◪ 40-60
▨ 60 and over

Source: M. El-Ashry and D. Gibbons, *Troubled Waters* 8 (World Resources Inst. Study 6, Oct. 1986).

Average annual precipitation in the coterminous United States.

This stupendous transformation of the western landscape is palpable and real, but in another sense it is an illusion. It can be sustained only as long as the water holds out. The modern American West could be likened to a great, rich, serious-minded Disneyland—most of its wealth, most of its population, its very existence dependent on the artificial manipulation of water in thousands of dams and tens of thousands of miles of aqueducts and canals.

What makes the West so fundamentally different from the country east of the hundredth meridian is its underlying hostility to the civilization that has been grafted onto it: the great hives of population, the crops genetically accustomed to 30 or 40 (or 80) annual inches of rain. As such, the modern West, from the booming Sunbelt cities to the prodigious harvests of the San Joaquin Valley, is haunted by the vulnerability all desert civilizations have shared throughout history. If you dynamited the levees along the Mississippi River, you would lose New Orleans. Destroy the biggest dams, change the climate, and you devastate the modern West.

To westerners, this is, perhaps, belaboring the obvious. But few easterners appreciate how important water is in the western states. As the Eskimo culture has a couple of dozen subtly different words meaning "snow" and "ice," a whole vocabulary of water exists in the West that the rest of the country does not readily understand. Water does not flow down rivers; it "wastes." The "conservation" of water means building dams. The world of western water is peopled by appropriators and diverters who have been granted senior and junior rights, by state engineers and water masters who wield the powers of star tribunals. Water may be Type I or II, Class One or Two, first use or return flow, surface water or conjunctive use water, discrete groundwater or perched groundwater. An obscure and complex corpus of law has grown up around water, with certain tenets an easterner might find bizarre. Steal your neighbor's water for a few years and get away with it, and the water is yours. Leave your water in a stream (even if your intended use demands that it remain there), and you may lose it. Take it out, for nearly any purpose, and it is almost always "beneficial" use. And, of course, the ultimate law of western water is that it always flows uphill—toward money.

Because water, scarce and indispensable as it is, long ago achieved holiness in the American West, the *development* of water has qualified as a secular religion during most of its history. Westerners may have fought over dams and water rights—state versus state, basin versus basin, farmer versus city, neighbor versus neighbor—but to oppose water development *in principle* (as John Muir did in Hetch Hetchy Valley and David Brower did in Glen Canyon and Echo Park) is the worst kind of heresy. Water development is an unqualified good, and the cause of water development transcends party affiliation and ideology— and, according to critics, reason and common sense. Senator

Ernest Gruening, nominally a conservationist, could strongly favor what would have been the largest reservoir in the world—a reservoir that would have completely submerged Alaska's most spectacular waterfowl habitat—just as Barry Goldwater, the prototypical antifederal conservative, could ardently support the Central Arizona Project, which is as close to socialism as anything the federal government has ever done. Perhaps nothing better symbolizes the West's love affair with water development than the inscription in the great arch welcoming visitors to Modesto, California: "Water, Wealth, Contentment, Health."

The arch is still there, its inscription the same, but in recent years the West's infatuation with dam-building and aqueducts has obviously soured. Many westerners no longer believe that more water development "solves" anything in the long run, just as new freeway lanes are no answer to traffic congestion and more police are not necessarily the solution to crime. New dams have also become extremely expensive, and with the federal government no longer willing to pay the entire cost, a lot of people wonder whether the investment is worthwhile. And, more and more, westerners have begun to rue the environmental costs of water development: the extinct salmon runs, the drastic decline in wildlife (particularly waterfowl) habitat, the canyons drowned by bathtub reservoirs, the poisoned and depauperated rivers.

Such revisionist thinking may be more prevalent in Oregon and California than in, say, Idaho and Utah. Nonetheless, between environmental opposition, public apathy or indecisiveness, increasingly unbearable costs, and some success with water transfers and conservation, dam construction throughout the West, after going at breakneck speed since the 1920s, has been at a virtual standstill for the past ten years. (Most of the available construction funds are being used to finish long-authorized projects.)

How long this can continue is a fascinating question. The water situation in the West is, up to a point, strikingly similar to the national energy picture. Despite very modest new energy facility construction and stable domestic oil production, an energy crisis has, in spite of predictions, failed to materialize. One important reason is the almost madcap binge of new power plant construction that went on in the 1960s and 1970s, when projections of future demand were far higher than demand turned out to be. In the case of water, the West has been living on surpluses, too—enormous quantities made available from the 1950s to the 1970s, when the Central Valley and State Water projects in California, Glen Canyon Dam in Arizona, and dozens of smaller projects were completed.

But a second—and probably more significant—reason for low *energy* demand growth is that our appetite for oil and electricity has been greatly curbed. Through market mechanisms (higher cost means greater efficiency) and tough federal laws, automobiles, appliances, office buildings, and virtually everything else that requires energy uses much less of it than fifteen years ago. Automobile fuel efficiency has nearly doubled; the best modern refrigerators use only a third as much energy as their predecessors. By one estimate, our success with energy conservation saves us the equivalent of $150 billion worth of imported oil each year.

In the case of western water, unfortunately, no such savings has occurred. The whole system encourages inefficient use. Federal water subsidies, hydropower subsidies, crop subsidies, the doctrine of appropriative rights, constraints on water transfers, fixed or declining block rates—a whole gamut of conservation disincentives has given the American West the most prodigious thirst of any desert civilization on earth. These inefficiencies persist, in part, because of a feeling (at least among water planners and engineers) that when shortages do occur, the construction juggernaut will inevitably roll again.

Is that possible or likely? Would it be economical or wise? Are there even rivers left to dam up? Or can the West's impending water shortages be solved by more efficient use? For how long? Where do you begin encouraging more efficient use, and where do you stop? What laws and policies would you change or scrap? What kinds of social and economic pain will be felt if the booming urban regions begin sucking the agricultural lands dry? On the other hand, what is western agriculture worth—economically, culturally, or by any other measure—compared to the water it consumes? What of the environmental damage

7

that water development has caused—salts and selenium in water and soil, poisoned wildlife refuges, vanishing salmon runs
and estuarine productivity? How much damage is preventable
or reparable, and at what cost?

The idea of this book is to take a somewhat brief, mostly dispas-
sionate, look at these issues and offer what Jonathan Swift
might have called a modest proposal for reforming water policy
in the American West. Our major emphasis must be on federal
policy. After all, the U.S. government—mainly through the Bureau of Reclamation and Army Corps of Engineers, but also
through federally arranged compacts and congressional legislation—has long been the most important single player in western water affairs. The Bureau of Reclamation controls far more
water than anyone else in the West; it sells the cheapest and
some of the most inefficiently used water around; and great new
dams and aqueducts, if any are built, are apt to be initiated and
largely funded by the bureau or the corps. (A few municipal
water agencies, notably the Denver Water Board and the East
Bay Municipal Utility District in Oakland, are planning huge
dam projects, too.) Moreover, federal policies not specifically
oriented toward water could have an enormous impact on water
use. The Department of Agriculture's Conservation Reserve program is a notable example, as are various crop subsidy and set-
aside programs and laws such as the Clean Water Act.

On the other hand, the federal water development agencies
generally must abide by the strictures of state water law, and
these codes vary in important ways from one western state to
the next. In Colorado, water is basically a free commodity that
can be bartered, leased, and sold—within limits. In California,
redistributing water or water rights has been much more difficult. Some states have passed laws to create minimal instream
flows for fish, wildlife, and recreation; others have refused.
Therefore, we will also examine the water codes of the eleven
western states (we exclude Alaska and Hawaii); our purpose is to
illuminate strengths and weaknesses and to suggest where laws
or language might be changed.

As all authors do, we bring certain biases to this study even as
we strain to be objective. Perhaps it is best to confess them right

away. First, we take it as given that concern about the environment, and about husbanding the nation's natural resource base, is not a passing fad but a permanent and powerful new reality in American political life—one we wholeheartedly endorse. Today's water development policies, for the most part, reflect an entirely different era when growth and economic development were the West's paramount concerns and environmental values were given short shrift. We believe that a vast majority of Americans, given a choice, would insist on greater sensitivity to the environment in future water planning and development. We also believe that particularly egregious damage—the enormous loss of western wetlands acreage, for example—ought to be reversed to some degree. Obviously, we cannot restore 4.5 million acres of wetlands to California. But we can support changes in state water codes, and in federal water pricing and policies, that could discourage further losses of wetlands and create incentives to restore some of these vanished ecological treasures.

We also take it as given that profound economic and social changes have occurred in the West since World War II. The West is a much more urban society today, even though agriculture still consumes the lion's share of the water in every western state. Water consumed in an urban setting usually generates more wealth than water used to irrigate crops. Recognizing this as fact does not, however, mean that one undervalues the economic or, perhaps more important, the social and cultural value of agriculture.

And, finally, it is hard to argue with the assertion that water is the most artificially regulated natural resource (except, perhaps, for uranium) in the West. For decades the sale and distribution of water have been removed, by varying degrees, from free market principles governing other resources such as coal, timber, and land itself. Bureau of Reclamation water, in particular, is sometimes locked into current uses at the same time it is deeply subsidized, creating severe distortions in what purports to be a free market economy. We would like to see some of these constraints removed and the subsidies reduced or phased out—to advocate market principles requires no apology. On the other hand, we recognize that doing so could cause hardship to certain communities, especially those whose prosperity has been based

9

on the continuous availability of cheap irrigation water. If government intervention was necessary to get us where we are, then further intervention, but of a different nature, may be needed to get us smoothly where we ought to go.

In short, to the degree that authors may editorialize to support their prejudices, we would favor more environmental protection, not less; we would favor less regulation, not more. But we also recognize that stronger environmental protection may demand more regulation. We would like to see the principles of the free market applied to water in the West, but certainly not in every instance. The United States has never had a pure free market economy, nor would most Americans want one—and where a resource as scarce and important as western water is concerned, free market mechanisms may be hard to apply for the greater good of all.

These prejudices, caveats, and clarifications aside, we have tried to present a fair assessment. Readers may accuse us of bias or of making recommendations too weak or too tough. We hope we cannot be accused of insensitivity.

Part I ▬▬▬▬▬▬▬▬▬▬

A Brief Look at
Western Water History

THE American West was explored and settled by the Spanish
just half a century after Columbus made landfall, and long before the Jamestown colony and Plymouth Rock. For the next
three centuries, however, its colonization proceeded much more
slowly than in the East. One reason was distance, but perhaps an
equally important one was water. Had the polarities of climate
been reversed—had the East been semiarid to arid and the West
humid to wet—the landless European masses might well have
risked the trip around Cape Horn, and the continental cross-
migration could have gone in reverse.

Among all Europeans, the Spanish were best suited to try to
build a civilization in the West; they were used to semiarid
climates and experienced with irrigation. But the West was
much different from Spain. Outside of California and Arizona,

11

the climate is considerably colder, and where there is year-round warmth the West tends to be emphatically dry. Moreover, even though much of Spain receives less than 20 inches of rainfall per year, as California does, precipitation tends to come year-round. California is virtually rainless during most of the growing season. Not just irrigation but *constant* irrigation was critical to survival. Since Spain was singular in its approach to colonization—its missionaries served as its settlers' advance men—Indians were desperately needed to help with all the work. But the California Indians, who as hunters and gatherers were utterly unused to such labor and drudgery, tended to rebel and depart, offenses which were severely punished. Punishment made the Indians more hostile, and a vicious cycle was begun. Most historians have attributed Spain's bewildering loss of interest in the Southwest to its failure to find precious metals. It is just as plausible, however, that the Spanish were drawn to a region that reminded them of home—and then proved to be a far tougher place to settle.

The settlers of northern European origin who were lured from the East by the expansionist railroads ("Rain follows the plow!," the meteorological fraud of the century, was their clarion call) and the homestead acts learned the same lesson, only more painfully, as they trespassed into the continent's arid zone and began planting their farms on the western plains. The land boom had been on for barely twenty years (most of them unusually wet) when the Great White Winter of 1886 struck, followed by the drought of 1888–1892. Kansas and Nebraska saw their populations decline by nearly one-half. By 1893, of a million families who had tried to settle the semiarid plains, only 400,000 remained.[1] Farther east, farmers had to cut down great virgin hardwoods, yank out the stumps, and clear rubbly, rock-strewn fields; but the homestead acts, despite their promise of virtually rockless and treeless, fertile land, were for the most part a dismal failure west of the hundredth meridian.

---

[1] For a good account of the western settlers' terrible difficulties see Wallace Stegner, *Beyond the Hundredth Meridian* (Houghton Mifflin, 1953).

The Inevitable Federal Role

Many of the western settlers who prevailed were those who had established homesteads along rivers and streams and begun to irrigate. In the public imagination, irrigation had been consigned to warmer climates like California's—and to the Mormons—but after Horace Greeley established a successful, non-Mormon irrigation colony north of Denver, interest in this novel type of farming heightened considerably. Scores of private irrigation companies were formed with eastern capital, stocked with eastern engineers, and sent West to subdue the desert. Cooperative irrigation districts were stitched together among landowners. By the early 1890s, some 3.5 million acres had come under irrigation in the West.

That achievement, unfortunately, was not nearly as impressive as it seems. Mormons were responsible for at least half the acreage; their diligence, social cohesiveness, and sheer obstinate will made them difficult to emulate. Most of the rest was in Southern California and along such rivers as the South Platte and Arkansas, whose waters were easily diverted and stored in natural offstream basins for summertime use. (Much of the conservation storage on the plains is still provided by these same playa basins, instead of by mountain reservoirs.) But most western topography is not like that of the plains. The rivers tend to flow in canyons, and in order to regulate and divert their waters one has to build large dams—a task beyond the means and ability of nearly all the early private companies and cooperatives.

The results were predictable. At the eighth National Irrigation Congress in 1898, one speaker compared the western landscape to a graveyard, littered by the "crushed and mangled skeletons of defunct irrigation companies . . . which suddenly disappeared at the end of brief careers, leaving only a few defaulted obligations to indicate the route by which they departed."[2] In some regions, the collapse of private-cooperative irrigation ventures was economically calamitous. When the Newlands Project in

---

[2] Quoted in M. Reisner, *Cadillac Desert* (Viking-Penguin, 1986), p. 116.

Nevada went bust (mainly because of political interference by the legislature and squabbles among the settlers) at the end of the silver boom of the 1870s and 1880s, Francis Newlands, the chief sponsor and funder of the project, announced, "Nevada is a dying state."[3] In fact, the population exodus from Nevada at that time, expressed as a percentage of those who remained, is still the greatest in American history.

Nonetheless irrigation, or "reclamation," by the late nineteenth century, had attained the status of a movement with a well-organized constituency (the National Reclamation Association and other groups) and strong political support in various quarters. Belatedly recognizing the shortcomings of the eastern-oriented homesteading legislation, Congress tried to align the terms and conditions of subsequent legislation with the realities of western climate—also without much success. The Desert Land Act of 1877 offered 640-acre tracts in the western states and territories to anyone who promised to irrigate them in three years; the standards of "proof" were so lax that the act's main result was speculation on an almost heroic scale. The Carey Act of 1894 authorized the federal government to donate land to states for the purpose of irrigation farming, but the states proved no more competent at building reservoirs, finding suitable soils, and mastering irrigation's complex art than the worst of the private companies. Over sixteen years, the Carey Act was responsible for bringing only 288,000 acres under irrigation, some of the time.

By the turn of the century, it had finally become clear that irrigation would achieve very limited success without a far more prominent federal role. As it happens, the nation's political history was at a juncture that made such a role possible. The progressive movement was gathering strength, a reaction against unfettered capitalism and the social chaos and political corruption it had wrought. Theodore Roosevelt, the incoming president, had lived in the West and owned a scientific mind that understood the formidable obstacles to settlement posed by climate and terrain. Roosevelt was not frightened by federal powers and, moreover, was anxious to build up America's weak

---

[3] Ibid.

western flank. And Francis Griffith Newlands, who lost half a million dollars in his irrigation venture, was now a congressman who could testify eloquently before his colleagues about the limitations of private enterprise. Everything else had been tried, and with some notable exceptions nothing had worked. Like the Civil Rights and Clean Air Acts, the Reclamation Act of 1902 is enshrined in that special category of legislation marked "inevitable."

How the Government Watered the West

The Reclamation Act represents—in theory if not always in reality—the application of a Hamiltonian means (strong centralized government) in pursuit of Jeffersonian ends: the preservation and expansion of rural life and rural values, local democracy, and a landed middle class.

A powerful central government has been a fact of American political life for so long that it is hard to appreciate what a radical piece of legislation the Reclamation Act was in its day. At a time when the president was—or had been—something more than a figurehead, it handed remarkable new powers to the executive branch, allowing a presidential appointee, the secretary of the interior, to choose locales where a great deal of federal money would be invested and where, as a result, rapid population growth and economic development were likely to occur. At a time when much of the nation's road system was still privately owned and maintained, it suddenly authorized the federal government to build huge, expensive dams.

When it came to economic principles, moreover, the Reclamation Act represented a complete departure from the norm. Project beneficiaries would be charged enough for water (again, in theory) to repay the government's capital costs, but they would be exempted from repaying interest on the government's investment. It was exactly as if the government loaned someone money for a house interest-free. Some critics have called the act, acerbically but probably correctly, the nation's first piece of welfare legislation for the common man.

15

The key provisions of the original act were as follows: A dam site would be chosen and a reclamation district, or water service area, would be designated within the watershed. The government would design and build the dams and canals and associated works; the irrigation districts and farmers would themselves be responsible for getting the water to their land. No one could legally farm more than 160 acres with subsidized reclamation water; recordable contracts were required so that this provision could be enforced. To discourage absentee ownership, farmers were required to live within 50 miles of their land.

As far as some of the Reclamation Act's detractors were concerned, the interest-free provision was an unwarranted, if not outrageous, subsidy. In reality, however, it was not subsidy enough—at least so long as a ten-year repayment period remained law. Even sponsors such as Newlands and Roosevelt failed to appreciate how expensive irrigation—a profoundly unnatural act—can be. All agriculture is really a battle against nature, but once an eastern farmer had cleared his land of rocks and trees, his major battles were won; he merely had to be frugal, work extremely hard, and pray for rain. In most cases, irrigation farming calls for river regulation, which means dams, which can involve enormous expense. Then the farmers must build, or pay for, canals and ditches that may cost even more. But even then the battle is not won. Canals and laterals are inclined to silt up and fall into disrepair. Accumulated salts must be leached out of the soil; underground drains must sometimes be installed to prevent the increasingly saline water table from rising into the root zones of the crops. That many of the early reclamation farmers had no experience with irrigation agriculture did not help—nor did the Reclamation Service's inclination to build the dams and canals and leave the farmers to fate.

For these and other reasons, a majority of the reclamation farmers were soon defaulting on their repayment obligations. As a result, the act began to undergo a long and remarkable series of adjustments, commonly referred to as reforms. In 1906, it was amended to allow sales of subsidized hydroelectricity to farmers and unsubsidized power to nearby towns. In 1914, the repayment term was finally stretched out to twenty years. Even so, by

1922 some 60 percent of the reclamation farmers—now a significant minority among the rural population of the West—were
still in default. Two years later, Congress commissioned a so-
called Fact Finder's Report to put the program on a stable foot-
ing once and for all; the main result was that the repayment
period was doubled again, this time to forty years. (Later a ten-
year "grace" period was added, making it effectively fifty years.)
But many farmers, especially those in high-altitude states
(where mainly low-value crops such as alfalfa are grown), were
still unable to make a profit and repay the government on the
proceeds of 160 acres—so, under a more liberal interpretation of
the act, the limit was revised to 320 acres for a man and wife.
And in some special cases, repayment periods were stretched
out, through congressional action, to seventy and eighty years.[4]

The motivation for all this legislation was humane, as were
the results: The adjustments allowed tens of thousands of hard-
working citizens to remain on their land. But in another sense,
the adjustments to the act deserve comparison with the renego-
tiation of Latin American debt and the bailout of savings and
loan institutions: They permitted dubious federal investments
to continue, encouraged more of them, and made the taxpayers
the rescuers of last resort.

Meanwhile, a subtle but profound ideological change was
hurrying the reclamation program along. Prior to 1902, much of
the opposition to the Reclamation Act had come, ironically,
from the West; many westerners saw it, however quixotically, as
unwarranted federal interference in their affairs. But by the late
1920s, the whole region was clamoring for more projects, and
politicians posturing as enemies of government were lobbying
frantically to bring more projects home. Herbert Hoover, who
abhorred strong central government and social welfare programs, was also a westerner; he laid the groundwork for not just
Boulder (later Hoover) Dam but for Grand Coulee, as well, a
project most conservatives loathed. When it came to water development, party affiliation and ideology mattered less and less.

It was the New Deal, however, that shifted the reclamation
program—and the entire federal public works bureaucracy—

---

[4] Michael Robinson, *Water for the West* (Public Works Historical Society, 1979).

into high gear. The Roosevelt administration's first priority was to stimulate the nearly paralyzed economy; the quickest and surest approach was to build public works; and the agencies already in business whose business was public works were the Bureau of Reclamation and the Army Corps of Engineers. By 1936, just four years after FDR took office, the world witnessed what ranks, even today, as civil engineering's finest hour: The five largest modern structures on the planet—Hoover, Bonneville, Fort Peck, Shasta, and Grand Coulee dams—were all going up at the same time. In the East, the Tennessee Valley Authority broke every kind of record by building twenty large dams on the Tennessee River and its major tributaries in twenty years. The Corps of Engineers, meanwhile, was embarking on a reservoir construction program that erected ten large dams a year, on average, for fifty years. In 1944, Congress authorized nearly 300 Missouri Basin projects (the Pick-Sloan program) at a single stroke!

This was no longer "orderly" development, a favorite phrase in the water planners' vocabulary; it was headlong, almost manic development. There were several motivations behind it. One, obviously, was the Depression and Roosevelt's secret fear that periodic economic collapse was capitalism's fatal, self-destructive weakness. As one historian noted, "New Deal planners viewed natural resources primarily as an essential element of general economic planning, necessary to mitigate the effects of the Depression, accomplish recovery, and prevent future depressions." According to this same historian, New Deal planners held "an almost religious belief in the value of public hydroelectric power development."[5] Economies of scale figure prominently in the economics of hydroelectricity, high dams produce much more power than low dams, and many reclamation projects required hydroelectric subsidies; that is another reason why so many dams—especially large, high dams—were built and planned under the New Deal.

But the most important reason was simply that public works were phenomenally popular. As awed members of Congress

---

[5] U.S. Department of Agriculture, Economic Research Service, *A History of Federal Water Resources Programs, 1800–1960* (June 1972), p. 13.

watched Roosevelt in action, and heard their constituents compare him favorably with God, Congress's grip on the public purse went limp. The initial Public Works Administration appropriation for Grand Coulee Dam was the largest single-purpose peacetime appropriation in United States history. Some hydrologists still wonder exactly what purpose is served by Montana's Fort Peck Dam—even today the fourth largest dam on the planet, on a river not yet grown to middling size—but Congress seems to have approved it without a second thought. The Depression changed the public's (and therefore Congress's) attitude toward public works as nothing else could have; the Dust Bowl made everyone believe in water development all the more. Roosevelt was also the greatest communicator who ever sat in the Oval Office; enormously persuasive himself, he understood the importance of public relations as no previous president had. In the 1940s, for example, he appointed the Bureau of Reclamation's director of public affairs, Michael Straus, as commissioner. Straus, like his two immediate superiors—Interior Secretary Harold Ickes and Assistant Secretary William Warne—was a former newspaper and public relations man, so in love with water development that one of his successors as commissioner, Floyd Dominy, would later observe that "facts didn't mean a God-damned thing to him." As such, the reclamation program became less the province of conservative, cautious engineers than the domain of super-salesmen.[6]

The New Deal leadership's irrepressible exuberance concerning public works, combined with the Depression and the Great Drought (and, one should add, the catastrophic levee-topping Mississippi River flood of 1928, which transformed the Corps of Engineers from a skeptic into an enthusiastic proponent of flood control reservoirs), might have been enough to launch the water development agencies on a forty-year binge. But they were greatly assisted by several key pieces of legislation passed by Congress during the Roosevelt and Truman administrations.

One was the Flood Control Act of 1936, which effectively launched a national flood control program under the jurisdiction of the Corps of Engineers. An outgrowth of a 1934 National

---

[6] Reisner, *Cadillac Desert.*

Resources Board recommendation that water planning should be done basin-wide rather than on a project-by-project basis, the act led to river-basin "planning" in all the larger western watersheds and to the authorization, through subsequent legislation, of dozens of basin-wide projects at a single stroke. (The Pick-Sloan program, authorized by the Flood Control Act of 1944, is the most notable example.)[7]

Just as important was the Reclamation Project Act of 1939, which authorized the interior secretary to plan and construct projects for purposes in addition to reclamation. These included navigation, flood control, municipal water supply, public sales of hydroelectricity, and recreation—all of which have figured importantly, if not decisively, in benefit/cost calculations for marginal irrigation dams.

Benefit/cost analysis itself was an outgrowth of Section I of the Flood Control Act of 1936, which stated that projects should be built only "if the benefits to whomsoever they may accrue are in excess of the estimated costs." Critics charge that this provision, like much well-meaning legislation, has been flagrantly abused to justify projects which could not withstand an honest analysis. (Retired high-level officials of the bureau have admitted as much in interviews.) The real significance of this provision is that it has given federal water resources development an aura of economic high-mindedness, even if the economic analyses performed by both the bureau and the Corps of Engineers have sometimes been dishonest and self-serving.[8]

As far as the Bureau of Reclamation is concerned, perhaps no development was more auspicious for the construction of new dams than the river-basin "accounting" method adopted in the early 1940s. It is not clear what legislation authorized this novel approach to bookkeeping: Some critics think it is merely a convenient perversion of the river-basin "planning" methodology authorized by the Flood Control Act of 1936. Through river-basin accounting, the bureau began tossing all revenues from power and irrigation features in a given watershed into a com-

---

[7] USDA, *A History of Federal Water Resources Programs.*

[8] See, in particular, excerpts from a long interview with Daniel Dreyfus, former chief of planning for the Bureau of Reclamation, in Reisner, *Cadillac Desert,* chap. 8 (especially pp. 302–303).

mon pool, not distinguishing between the money-making ventures (chiefly hydroelectric power) and the money-losing ones
(mainly irrigation projects). Besides hiding the losers among the
winners, river-basin accounting was mainly responsible for the
"cash register dam": a power-producing feature whose main
raison d'être is to subsidize failing irrigation projects. (Cash register dams were made technically legal by the multiple-purpose
language in the Reclamation Project Act of 1939.) Glen Canyon
Dam is in many respects a cash register dam; the two dams
which the bureau planned to build in the Grand Canyon in the
1960s would have served *only* to subsidize water sales to central
Arizona farmers and finance a future transbasin diversion to
augment the depleted Colorado River.

Thus, by the 1940s, the federal reclamation program had come
an extraordinary distance from its early, feeble origins.
Stretched-out repayment periods, multiple-purpose legislation,
and subsidies provided by hydroelectric power revenues all
served, or conspired, to justify projects which would not have
passed muster under the original terms of the Reclamation Act.
River-basin planning could authorize dozens of projects at once;
river-basin accounting could make them appear worthwhile.
The reclamation program enjoyed tremendous public support
because millions of people owed their livelihood to it; millions
of others (many of them city dwellers) received its water and
electricity. Federally sponsored water development had made a
number of construction companies—Bechtel, Morrison-
Knudsen, and Brown and Root among them—huge and rich,
and they handsomely rewarded the members of Congress who
supported the bills that gave them work, creating what
amounted to a public works oligarchy in Congress.[9] The result
was an unprecedented, thirty-year water development binge
unrivaled even by Brazil's feverish pace of construction in the
Amazon Basin today.

By the 1960s, however, the tide had already begun to turn
against the bureau and the corps. Under Floyd Dominy, who
served as commissioner for most of that decade, the bureau

---

[9] For a good discussion of the rise of one such company, Brown and Root, and the
politicians who made it possible, see Robert Caro, *LBJ: The Path to Power* (Knopf,
1985).

squandered much of its public reputation on a fruitless but hammerheaded campaign to build dams in the Grand Canyon, winning it the wrath of such publications as *My Weekly Reader* and *Reader's Digest*. As the best dam sites were used, the bureau was forced to look to more marginal projects: A very expensive dam might irrigate substandard or problem-plagued cropland whose production was likely to be further subsidized by federal price supports. (The Westlands Water District, irrigated by the San Luis Project, is an almost too-perfect example.) By spending more and more for less and less, the bureau became a target not just of powerful eastern members of Congress (Senator Paul Douglas of Illinois and Congressman John Saylor of Pennsylvania were two of the more notable examples) but of cost cutters in the executive branch itself, especially the Bureau of the Budget (later, and more authoritatively, reincarnated as the Office of Management and Budget). The progressive extinction of free-flowing rivers and waterfowl wetlands at the hands of reclamation dams and farms, and the Corps of Engineers' inveterate flood-control and drainage work, infuriated many sportsmen, some of them both wealthy and powerful. President Dwight Eisenhower had already tried, fruitlessly, to enforce a policy of "no new project starts," but under Presidents Nixon and Ford, and even New Dealer Lyndon Johnson, some projects were successfully delayed and undermined by the executive branch. The death or political retirement of powerful congressional allies such as Carl Hayden of Arizona, Bernard Sisk of California, and Wayne Aspinall of Colorado also contributed to the reclamation program's malaise.

But it was the growing power of the environmental movement, coinciding with the election of President Jimmy Carter, that really threw a wrench in the works. Environmental organizations had earlier helped lobby into existence several pieces of legislation, notably the National Environmental Policy Act, that made life more difficult for the water agencies; they were now compelled to consider and publicize the environmental consequences of their work. If an agency failed to prepare an environmental impact statement (EIS), which could take months or years, it was routinely sued; if an environmental organization considered an EIS inadequate—nearly always—it was routinely sued again. Thus the courts played an important (if reluctant) role in applying the brakes to water development, ordering projects delayed in highly inflationary times; after four or five or ten years of protracted litigation, costs had often doubled or tripled, and Congress—which now had outspoken and fairly powerful environmentalists in its ranks—frequently denied sufficient funds to get projects built soon. (Nearly $300 million has been dribbled out for preconstruction work on California's Auburn Dam, authorized many years ago, but work on the dam itself has not even begun.)

Then Jimmy Carter, who made plain his feeling that the federal water resources program was in need of reform—reform that would result in fewer projects, not more—attacked the program on all fronts almost from the day he took office, including nearly two dozen major projects on a "hit list." He achieved more sound and fury than results, but made a major national controversy out of water development probably for the first time since the debate over the Reclamation Act.

A few thousand dead waterfowl, however, probably discredited the federal water resources program with more thumping effect than all Carter's criticism and the environmental movement ever did. In the early 1980s, biologists at California's Kesterson National Wildlife Refuge discovered whole rafts of ducks, coots, and other birds dying of some mysterious malady—one that induced not just lethargy and eventual death but gruesome embryonic deformities. Ducks were being hatched without feet and with brains protruding from their heads. The cause was almost certainly selenium, a toxic metal which had leached into the refuge from surrounding farm fields in the Westlands Water District.

As far as the Bureau of Reclamation was concerned, a more inauspicious event could hardly have occurred at a more inauspicious place. The Westlands district had already achieved notoriety for its huge farm holdings receiving subsidized water illegally and for its plan—actually the bureau's and the state's—to build a vast, taxpayer-sponsored drain system that would discharge the brackish return flows into San Francisco Bay. (In fact, nearly one-third of the multi-billion-dollar cost was to be written off as a nonreimbursable wildlife benefit.) The Kesterson fiasco probably generated more national media coverage for the bureau than any event since the completion of Hoover Dam, virtually all of it negative. Congressman George Miller of California, one of the bureau's most persistent and powerful critics, likened it to someone pouring gasoline over himself. The tragedy at Kesterson did not inhibit Congress from expanding the acreage limitation sixfold in 1982, to 960 acres, but since the main lobbyist behind the Reclamation Reform Act was the Westlands Water District, that action probably damaged the bureau's reputation even more.[10] The vast majority of reclamation farmers irrigate holdings smaller than 960 acres, and the vast majority may not pour selenium-poisoned drainage into wildlife refuges. Yet, as far as a great many people are concerned, the reclamation program amounts to selling cheap taxpayer-subsidized water illegally to giant corporate farmers so they can poison wildlife refuges.

If the Carter administration's hostility toward water development shocked and infuriated many westerners, the Reagan administration's seeming lack of interest left them numb. Reagan's water development policy—which consisted of nine parts talk to one part action—may have slyly masked an antipathy (based on parsimony instead of environmental concern) no less heartfelt and truculent than Carter's. Whatever the case, with Interior Secretary James Watt suggesting that western water interests should pay "a third of the fare" for new projects; with William Clark, his successor, announcing that a San Joaquin Valley Master Drain is financially out of the question; and with their successor, Donald Hodel, inviting the Auburn Dam lobby to "buy the blueprints from the Bureau of Reclamation and build it yourselves,"[11] Reagan's position was clear: He was willing to finish some expensive projects, such as Central Arizona, but, like previous conservative Republicans in the White House, he did not seem to mind at all if no new dams were built during his term.

---

[10] Reisner, *Cadillac Desert;* see also D. Worster, *Rivers of Empire* (Pantheon Books, 1985).

[11] Hodel actually said this to the California Chamber of Commerce in 1987. He was also the first interior secretary to advocate the demolition of a long-standing dam: San Francisco's O'Shaughnessy, which flooded Hetch Hetchy Valley. In April 1989, Hodel, inexplicably, said he would try to get Auburn Dam *built.*

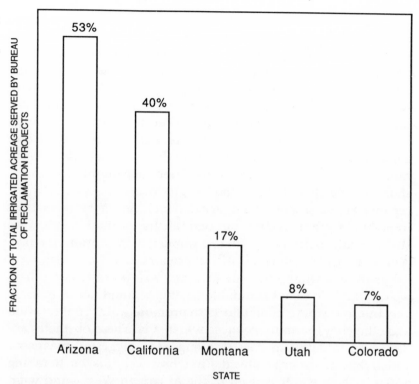

In selected western states the percentage of total irrigated acreage served by federal Bureau of Reclamation projects.

Clearly, then, in the past ten years the federal water resources program has suffered a series of reversals as stunning as the efflorescence of the New Deal era. Many factors have played a role: the scarcity of good dam and project sites, environmentalism, the federal deficit, surplus crop production, Kesterson, Westlands, fading memories of past droughts. The fascinating question is whether this moribundity will be permanent (or at least long-lived) or whether it is simply a brief hiatus before a new era of development begins. Diehard advocates of more development believe that America's refusal to build anew is a dismal mistake, some hydrological equivalent of our failure to match the German and Japanese rearmament preceding World War II. (Ironically, they have seized on one of environmentalism's favorite disaster scenarios—the Greenhouse Effect—as a rationale for more dams.) On the other hand, environmentalists and economists—among others—believe the West's developed water supply, more efficiently used, can satisfy urban and industrial growth and reasonable agricultural needs for many years.

Recently the Bureau of Reclamation—in what amounts to its most significant public utterance since its founding—announced that it will largely abandon its construction activities, at least for the foreseeable future, and metamorphose into a management-oriented agency. Exactly what the bureau has in mind is difficult to say, since it has been long on intentions and short on specifics. It has made vague pronouncements about repairing environmental damage and facilitating (or at least not impeding) water transfers, but real results, as of mid-1989, were still difficult to discern, with one important exception: the proposed lining of California's All-American Canal.

Regardless what the bureau plans to do—or what others would like it to do—formidable obstacles stand not only in its way but in the path of all efforts to promote water conservation and efficiency, no matter whose water it is. These obstacles are discussed in detail in Part II, along with suggested means by which they might be removed. First, however, it is worth taking a look at how water is used in the American West—and what that use has wrought both in positive and negative terms.

The Fruits of Water Development: A Balance Sheet

The modern western water system—dams, aqueducts, tunnels, canals, hydroelectric plants, and distribution infrastructure—is one of the region's most valuable assets, since little of its population, productive cropland, and economy could be sustained without it. Los Angeles' legendary water nabob, William Mulholland, calculated in 1904 that the metropolitan region had a local water supply sufficient to sustain only half a million people. Thanks to water imported from far beyond the basin, however, 13 million live there today in fake tropical splendor or squalor. Most of California's $16 billion in annual agricultural wealth is owed to irrigation; winter wheat and free-range livestock—about all that natural precipitation could support— would be worth a very small fraction of that amount. Though dryland agriculture and livestock raising are more important to other states than to California, much the same applies throughout the West.

About 60 million acres of land is currently being irrigated in the United States, a fifteenfold increase in the past century. Five-sixths of this acreage is in the seventeen western states. Of that total, some 9.9 million acres, or 20 percent, is directly irrigated by Bureau of Reclamation water. That figure, however, greatly undervalues the government's role in irrigating the West. For one thing, it does not include millions of acres protected from flooding or provided with regulated river flows courtesy of both Reclamation and Corps of Engineers dams. California's Tulare Lake, for example, was once the largest body of fresh water west of the Mississippi, but it has become a huge expanse of irrigated cropland since the Corps of Engineers dammed the four rivers flowing into it. Moreover, many reclamation farmers grew wealthy enough on federal irrigation to expand their acreage by pumping groundwater, just as some irrigation districts used the profits of federally subsidized irrigation to build their own supplemental projects. Thus federally supplied water has been both a creator of agricultural wealth and a catalyst to more of the same.

The Bureau of Reclamation's achievements as of 1987 are, from an engineering perspective, impressive indeed: 355 storage reservoirs, 254 diversion dams, 15,853 miles of canals, 1,376 miles of pipeline, 276 miles of tunnel, 37,263 miles of laterals, 17,002 miles of drainpipes and canals, and 51 hydroelectric plants with an installed capacity of 13.8 million kilowatts. The total federal investment in all of the above has been $9.4 billion, but since that figure represents uninflated dollars, and excludes most interest, the true value or opportunity cost is actually many times higher.

Bureau water deliveries in 1987 totaled 29.9 million acre-feet—25.5 million for irrigation, 3.2 million for municipal and industrial use, and 1.1 million for other nonagricultural use.

27

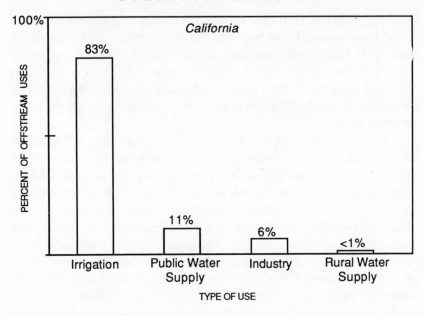

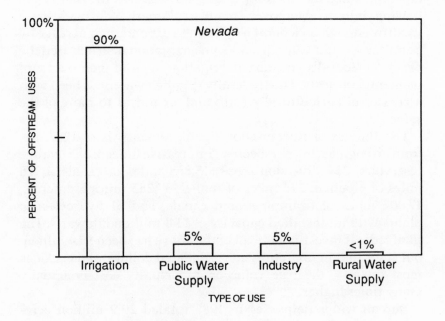

Out-of-stream water use patterns in various western states.

28

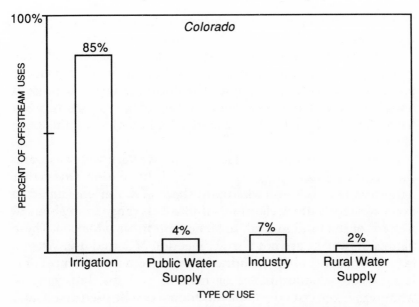

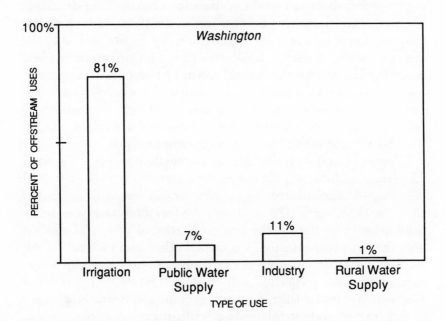

Some 25 million people were served by bureau water supplies, though much of this was supplemental water, not their main source. The gross value of all livestock and crops on lands irrigated by bureau water in 1987 was $8 billion, which amounted to 5.8 percent of farm value for the nation at large. Expressed another way, the gross annual value of all agriculture on federally irrigated lands is about equal to that of the state of Iowa.[12]

Three critically important facts about western water use, and the economy based on it, deserve careful elucidation. One is that irrigation uses the overwhelming share of water consumed in every western state. Irrigation withdrawals range from about 80 percent of the total in Utah to 90 percent in New Mexico. These figures, however, are not a true reflection of actual use. When a factory or power plant withdraws water from a river, most of it is returned—contaminated or heated, perhaps, but most of what was taken out goes back in. Often it can be used again, and again and again. The same applies to indoor domestic use, except the infinitesimal fraction used for cooking and drinking. The major *consumptive* uses of water in the West—which means that the water is evaporated, transpired by plants, or lost to the ocean or some unusable aquifer—are irrigating croplands and watering lawns. But the overall consumption of lawn watering, even in populous California, is as nothing compared to agriculture's. In California, agriculture consumptively uses about 90 percent of the state's water supply, compared with the 8 percent used by metropolitan Los Angeles (lawns and all).

In general, consumptive use for domestic purposes is around 25 percent of total withdrawals; for industrial purposes, 0 to 25 percent; for agriculture, 50 percent or higher. It is estimated that, in 1975, some 178 million acre-feet of water was withdrawn for irrigation in the United States, of which 97 million acre-feet was consumptively used. All other users withdrew 201 million acre-feet, but only 23 million acre-feet was effectively consumed. Thus irrigation, which is used on only 12 percent of the cropland in the United States, accounts for some 80 percent of U.S. urban, industrial, and agricultural water consumption.

[12] All these figures are taken from *1987 Summary Statistics*, vol. 1 (Denver: Bureau of Reclamation).

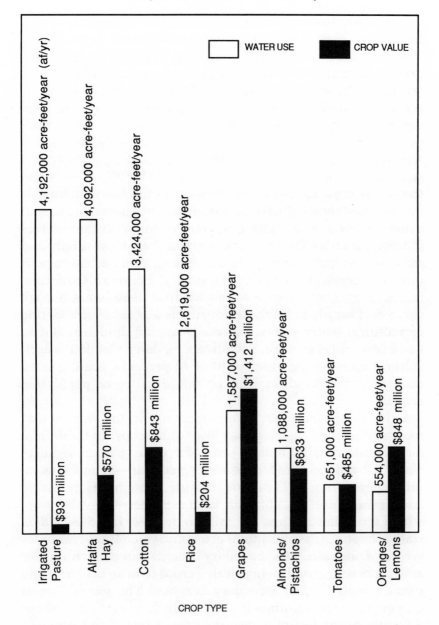

Total water use and crop value among selected crops grown in California (1986).

On the other hand, this same 12 percent of U.S. cropland produced over 25 percent of the *value* of all domestic crops.[13]

A second fact—already implicit in the figures just mentioned—is that continued rapid population growth in the arid West will not, in theory, overstrain the region's water supply. It is true that the West, contrary to common belief, is now the most urbanized region in the nation. Some 93 percent of California's population lives within designated metropolitan areas; even in New Mexico, the most rural western state, the figure is 42 percent. (It is 76 percent for the West as a whole.) The West is also the fastest-growing region in the nation, by far. But withdrawals for municipal and industrial purposes are still insignificant next to agriculture's. Some large cities not relying on distant sources of water, such as Tucson, have overrun their local supply and may have to build or tap into aqueducts; some urban regions utterly dependent on aqueducts, such as Southern California, face shortages in the near future because there is not enough developed supply to fill those aqueducts *and* satisfy competing agricultural water rights, especially during droughts. But in California and elsewhere, a relatively modest reduction in agricultural use—on the order of 10 or 12 percent—could free up enough water, in theory, to permit decades of population growth.[14]

A third important fact about water use in the West is that most agricultural water grows low-value crops. In California, for example, nearly 1 million acres of irrigated pasture requires about 4.2 million acre-feet of water per year—as much as an urban population of 23 million. Pasture, though it is the single largest water user in California, is an extremely low-value crop, with a gross value of just $93 million (in 1986) in a $480 *billion* state economy. (Pasture's total economic value is several times greater if one calculates secondary benefits, but a much smaller amount of water used on high-value crops or in an urban setting would produce equal secondary benefits.) The second-largest California water consumer is alfalfa, which, in 1986, used about 4.1 million acre-feet of water; the gross value of the crop was

---

[13] Interagency Task Force Report, *Irrigation Water Use and Management, 1979.*

[14] M. El-Ashry and D. Gibbons, *Troubled Waters: New Policies for Managing Water in the American West* (World Resources Institute, 1986).

only $570 million. Cotton, in third place with a total consumption of approximately 3.4 million acre-feet, had a gross value of $842 million. Irrigated rice used just over 2.6 million acre-feet and returned $204 million in gross value. These four crops accounted for nearly 50 percent of all agricultural water use in California.[15] By contrast, the value of California's grape crop— $1.5 billion—was almost equal to that of *all* the crops just mentioned, but the grape acreage used just 1.6 million acre-feet of water, about one-ninth as much.

Agriculture, while perhaps no longer the largest industry in California (defense, tourism, oil, and high technology are all in the same league), is certainly one of the most valuable contributors to the state's economy. It is also of considerable importance to the nation at large because it grows many of our specialty crops—avocados, artichokes, winter vegetables—and brings in considerable export income to help improve the country's imbalance of trade. But if, for the sake of argument, you entirely eliminated the pasture, alfalfa, cotton, and rice acreage—crops that can be grown on rainfall in numerous other states—and simply let the land revert to desert, you would free up enough water for 70 million new Californians (a 250 percent increase) while reducing total agricultural income by only 15 percent and shrinking the state economy by one-quarter of 1 percent. Eliminating *all* these crops would, of course, be both impossible and undesirable: Alfalfa is an important food for dairy cows, which are best raised locally; the San Joaquin Valley's desert climate grows an excellent, long-staple cotton that does not thrive as well in Louisiana or Mississippi. But such figures do demonstrate how much water is theoretically available for population growth at minimal economic cost; obversely, they demonstrate how much water is used to grow crops which are low-value, nonfood, or both.

What is true in California is even truer in other western states, because California's Mediterranean climate supports a huge acreage of high-value crops: oranges, lemons, almonds, walnuts, peaches, tomatoes, strawberries, carrots, lettuce, broccoli, as

---

[15] These figures, based on data from the Giannini Foundation and the Department of Water Resources, are available from the American Economic Association, Stanford University, Palo Alto, California.

paragus, and others that are grown commercially in few other states. Much the same applies to Arizona and the coastal portion of the Pacific Northwest: Crops that are both high in value and relatively thrifty with water are commonly grown. (Few orchard or row crops require as much water as alfalfa and pasture.) Throughout the rest of the West, however, this is emphatically *not* the case. At least 25 percent of all Colorado's available water is used to grow alfalfa, a crop which had a gross value of approximately $170 million in 1986.[16] Nevada's three main crops are hay, barley, and wheat; though irrigation withdraws 90 percent of the state's water, the crops it raised were worth only $46 million in 1986, a tiny sliver of the state's economy.[17]

From an economist's point of view, such patterns of water use—in a severely water-short region experiencing explosive urban growth—seem grotesquely inefficient. But there are usually historical reasons for inefficiency, and western water use is no exception. Before refrigeration and fast transportation, livestock had to be locally raised; hence farmers who got into the livestock business early were often granted extraordinarily generous water rights, which have been passed on through the generations. Moreover, when water costs $3 to $15 per acre-foot—as most federally supplied water does—even farmers in emphatically arid regions can afford to raise low-value crops. The Imperial Valley of California has the hottest climate in North America and receives just 2 or 3 inches of annual rainfall; annual waterings in excess of 7 acre-feet for alfalfa and 8 acre-feet for pasture are required. But figures for 1985 indicate that Imperial County raised 200,000 acres of alfalfa in that year—two-fifths of all the irrigated acreage in the county—in addition to 112,000 acres of grains and 6,200 acres of pasture.[18]

To be fair, one cannot measure the value of western agricultural water development simply by gross sales of agricultural commodities. Agriculture lends stability to the economies

---

[16] Personal communication with David Getches, former director of the Colorado Department of Natural Resources.

[17] *Nevada Statistical Abstract* (1988).

[18] California Department of Water Resources, Special Investigations, Imperial County Database (unpublished; sheet 12 of 58). Irrigation water use figures are taken from Department of Water Resources, *DWR Bulletin 160–83* (Sacramento, 1983).

of the more rural states—although this is far less true today than half a century ago. It is the lifeblood of many rural communities not built around tourism, mining, logging, or fishing. Agricultural water supply reservoirs—as well as urban ones—offer important economic benefits to farms, towns, and cities alike in their capacity to regulate floods. The Bureau of Reclamation has calculated that its California reservoirs prevented more than $5 billion in potential flood damage in 1986 alone, mainly by containing the floodwaters raised during an unprecedented ten-day storm which doused some Sierra Nevada watersheds with 50 inches of precipitation. That figure, however, is many times higher than it would have been in a normal year, and critics have persuasively challenged flood control benefits offered by both the Bureau of Reclamation and the Corps of Engineers. (Ironically, annual flood losses have been increasing despite the tens of billions spent on flood control; the main reason is that dams and levees have encouraged staggering investments in floodplain development on the false promise of total security.)[19]

Environmental Costs and Benefits

Assessing the environmental impact of federal water development in the West is not only difficult but an exercise in value judgment. To flatwater boaters and plug fishermen, a reservoir improves the natural environment; to whitewater boaters and stream fishermen, it degrades it. Hunters may look approvingly on irrigated mountain pasturelands and golf courses because they can be important food sources for deer—but the reservoir that waters such acreage may have drowned critically important winter habitat for deer, elk, or bighorn sheep.

More often than not, water development involves tradeoffs: the substitution of one form of recreation (speedboating versus rafting), habitat (rice fields versus wetlands), or wildlife species

---

[19] Environmental Policy Institute, *Disasters in Water Development II* (Washington, D.C., undated). The bureau's $5 billion flood control benefit figure is taken, without argument, from its *1987 Summary Statistics.*

(bass versus salmon) for another. Moreover, some projects have had impacts far more negative than others, making it difficult to generalize about the good or evil (in an environmental sense) that water development has caused. And to calculate the economic costs of water development (in lost salmon-fishing opportunities or whatever) is virtually impossible.

Nonetheless, one can argue that nothing has taken a greater toll on the natural heritage of the American West than reservoirs, aqueducts, and dams. The reservoirs themselves have submerged countless thousands of miles of superb scenery and native wildlife habitat; they have made a rarity of free-flowing streams. Meanwhile the water, diverted to other regions, has profoundly changed, often virtually obliterated, the natural features of the environment there.

An assessment of water development's impact on the natural environment of the West is worth a book in itself and, moreover, is not our purpose here. A quick overview of the damage caused by federal water development is worth including, however, since later we suggest some ways of reversing it. We do not propose to review the impacts of every project, or even the majority of them, but the most destructive should be mentioned.

The Columbia River Dams

Historically, the Columbia River was almost certainly the most prolific salmon-producing river in the world. Figures from the Northwest Power Planning Council suggest that the early-nineteenth-century runs of all five species migrating upriver to spawn totaled 10 to 16 million adult fish. (The Bonneville Power Administration's estimate is 35 million spawners!) Today, despite tens of millions of dollars invested in hatcheries, fish ladders, and similar mitigation, a relatively stable run of about 2.5 million fish is all that survives. Although the Columbia salmon run had already declined somewhat by World War I, due mainly to logging and overfishing, it was much greater than today's—and losses due to overfishing are usually reversible.

Since the construction of the Columbia River dams, however, the loss of more than 80 percent of the historic Columbia run has become an irreversible fact of life. Grand Coulee alone—which

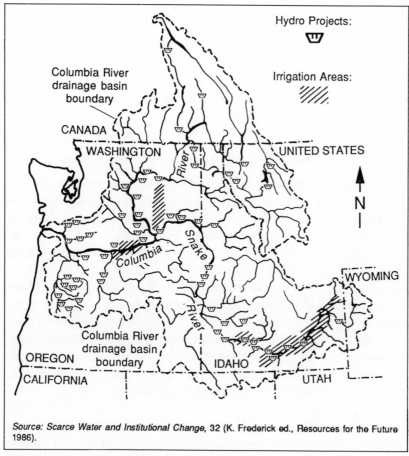

Hydro Projects: ♨

Columbia River drainage basin boundary

Irrigation Areas: ▨

CANADA
WASHINGTON
UNITED STATES

N

WYOMING

Columbia River drainage basin boundary

OREGON

IDAHO

CALIFORNIA

UTAH

Source: *Scarce Water and Institutional Change*, 32 (K. Frederick ed., Resources for the Future 1986).

Major dams and irrigation projects in the Columbia River Basin. Virtually undeveloped before the Depression, the Columbia Basin now has nearly sixty major dams.

is too high to be circumvented economically or even effectively by fish ladders—has blocked off access to nearly half of the watershed's historic spawning habitat. Even surmountable dams with fish ladders, such as Bonneville, confuse and delay countless thousands of fish, preventing many from spawning. And the dams are just as injurious to juvenile fish trying to reach the sea; countless billions are doomed to drift in slack reservoir waters or perish inside the whirling hydroelectric turbines.

Hatcheries have made up some of the loss, but not that much, and hatchery strains of fish are inferior to wild stock. Few works of man have had as profound an impact on a commercially valuable fishery as the Columbia system's thirty-odd dams. A species once so common that the men who worked on the dams demanded no more than three meals of salmon per week has become an expensive luxury.[20]

The Central Valley Project and Tulare Basin Dams

Thanks to a unique coincidence of climate and topography, the Central Valley of California, prior to its settlement by Europeans, stood comparison with the Serengeti region of East Africa. The vast, flat, imperceptibly sloping valley floor was an oak-studded blond grassland in the summer dry season which then metamorphosed, in large part, into a vast flourishing marsh in the winter and spring, when the flooding rivers of the Sierra Nevada overflowed their banks as they emerged from the foothills. Along the bigger rivers, stately forests of willows, cottonwoods, sycamores, and vine-draped oaks made a scene reminiscent of the virgin Southeast. In the early spring, the valley floor and lower foothills were so carpeted with wildflowers that "they seem to be painted"—so said John Muir.

At least as impressive as this gorgeous wild spectacle was the wildlife that called the valley its seasonal and permanent home. Antelope and tule elk were countless—a million of each species is a widely accepted figure. Thousands of grizzly bears roamed the valley floor and foothills, especially in the Coast Range. Millions of spawning salmon, silvers and chinooks, swam up the rivers year round (there were several seasonal runs) and crowded into tributary creeks. In the wintertime came the most impressive sight of all: skies almost overburdened with migrating ducks, geese, white pelicans, and sandhill cranes arriving from a great arc of summer habitat stretching from western Manitoba to Siberia. The primordial waterfowl numbers are impossible to estimate, but as late as the 1940s, after 80 percent

---

[20] Northwest Power Planning Council, *Compilation of Information on Salmon and Steelhead Losses in the Columbia River Basin* (Portland, March 1986); see chap. 2 of the report.

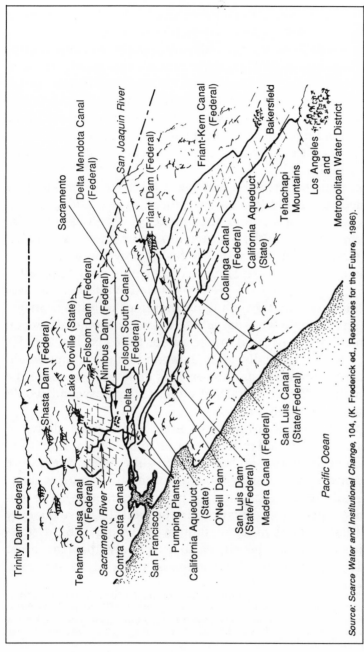

Trinity Dam (Federal)

Shasta Dam (Federal)

Tehama Colusa Canal (Federal)

Sacramento River

Contra Costa Canal

Lake Oroville (State)

Folsom Dam (Federal)

Nimbus Dam (Federal)

Folsom South Canal (Federal)

Delta

Sacramento

Delta Mendota Canal (Federal)

San Joaquin River

Friant Dam (Federal)

Friant-Kern Canal (Federal)

Bakersfield

San Francisco

Pumping Plants

California Aqueduct (State)

O'Neill Dam

San Luis Dam (State/Federal)

Madera Canal (Federal)

San Luis Canal (State/Federal)

Coalinga Canal (Federal)

California Aqueduct (State)

Tehachapi Mountains

Los Angeles and Metropolitan Water District

Pacific Ocean

Source: Scarce Water and Institutional Change, 104, (K. Frederick ed., Resources for the Future, 1986).

The Central Valley and State Water projects in California rank first and second among irrigation projects in the Western world. The State Water Project's California Aqueduct is 444 miles long; the Central Valley Project captures water sufficient for 40 million urban users, though nearly all of it goes to irrigation.

of the wetlands were already gone, nearly 50 million wintering waterfowl may have still come down.[21]

The antelope, tule elk, grizzly bear, and most other large mammalian species had largely or entirely vanished by the turn of the century. But even after decades of legal and illegal market hunting, commercial salmon fishing and poaching, and progressive habitat loss, waterfowl and anadromous fisheries remained relatively abundant and healthy until about World War II. Their downfall since then—and one cannot really call it anything else—has had much to do with federal dam and aqueduct construction and the irrigated acreage it fostered. Friant Dam, a centerpiece of the Central Valley Project, caused a large run of chinook salmon in the San Joaquin River to go extinct. The winter chinook run in the Sacramento River (the most productive salmon river in the state, by far) is now threatened with extinction, too—only a few hundred spawning adults are left— and the remaining runs are greatly reduced in numbers. Shasta Dam, a gigantic barrier sealing off hundreds of miles of prime salmon stream habitat, is largely to blame, although diversion dams and fish-killing canal intake pumps have also had a major impact. Whether these diversion dams and intake pumps would even exist without Shasta, however, is debatable, because the pre-dam flood flows of 400,000 cubic feet per second would likely have washed them away.[22]

Until the federal government erected its huge dams in California—the Bureau of Reclamation and Corps of Engineers have each built more than half a dozen—the major rivers were largely uncontrolled, even though dozens of tributary dams were already in place (mainly for power production). The federal dams, built at low elevations in the foothills, have not only cut off thousands of miles of salmon spawning habitat; they have also regulated the rivers so effectively that the great wetlands-nourishing flood flows almost never occur anymore.

---

[21] M. E. Heitmeyer et al., "The Central, Imperial, and Coachella Valleys of California," in L. Smith et al., *Habitat Management for Migrating and Wintering Waterfowl in North America* (Texas Tech Press, 1989). See also F. Smith, "The Changing Face of California's Central Valley" (U.S. Fish and Wildlife Service discussion paper, Sacramento, November 23, 1987).

[22] William Kier, California Salmon-Steelhead Advisory Committee, personal communication.

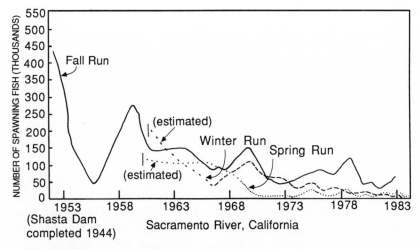

Source: California Salmon-Steelhead Advisory Committee

Remnant salmon runs in two important western rivers. Note that the Sacramento run is expressed in numbers of observed spawning fish; the Columbia run in pounds of landed fish. (The Sacramento River winter run of salmon is now listed as an Endangered Species by the state of California, with a surviving population of fewer than six hundred fish.)

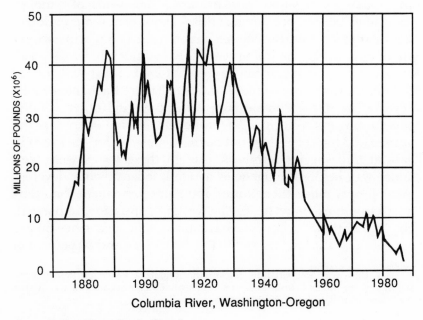

Source: Northwest Power Planning Council

Tulare Lake, for example, was once the largest continuous expanse of fresh water and wetlands in the state, but it has completely disappeared since the corps erected dams on all the rivers that once fed it. Several other nearby marshy lakes that attracted hundreds of thousands if not millions of waterfowl, as Tulare Lake did, are gone, too. Most California wetlands acreage is now artificially flooded with pumped groundwater or dependent on contaminated irrigation return flows.

Of the original 4 to 5 million acres of wetlands, only about 400,000 acres remain, mostly in private ownership; thousands more acres disappear every year. Wintering waterfowl populations have averaged only 3.5 million birds over the past ten years, compared to 10 million in the early 1970s and perhaps four times that number after World War II.[23]

Although fish and wildlife enhancement is an announced purpose in several amendments to the original Central Valley Project legislation, the Bureau of Reclamation supplies less than 100,000 acre-feet of firm (uninterruptible) fresh water to state and federal refuges in California—about 1.2 percent of the project's total supply.[24] Substantial return flows that began as federally developed water nurture some thousands of acres of waterfowl habitat, but much of this water is of dubious or downright wretched quality: The Kesterson tragedy is a prime example of how it may be doing waterfowl as much harm as good.

In summary, it seems fair to say that the Central Valley Project and the Corps of Engineers dams in Tulare Basin have had a devastating impact on salmon, waterfowl, and other wildlife populations in California. The minor mitigation offered by the bureau and the corps does not begin to make up for the losses in habitat and species numbers, though these losses were well under way before the agencies arrived; federal water development simply made them worse and more permanent than they might otherwise have been. The wetlands situation, in particular, is of national if not international significance, since 60 per cent of the waterfowl using the Pacific Flyway and 20 percent of

[23] U.S. Bureau of Reclamation, Mid-Pacific Region, *A Report on Refuge Water Supply Investigations, Central Valley Project Basin, California* (Sacramento, March 1989). See also Heitmeyer, "Valleys of California."

[24] Ibid.

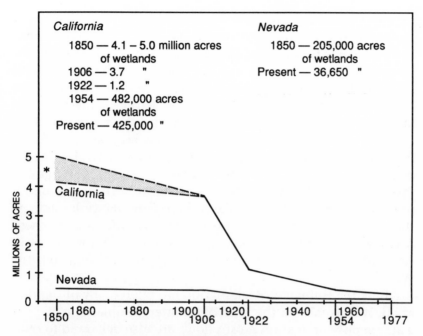

California

1850 — 4.1 – 5.0 million acres
of wetlands
1906 — 3.7 "
1922 — 1.2 "
1954 — 482,000 acres
of wetlands
Present — 425,000 "

Nevada

1850 — 205,000 acres
of wetlands
Present — 36,650 "

* Estimates prior to 1900 range from 4.1 to 5 million acres.

Wetland losses in California and Nevada, 1850–1977. (Losses due to contamination—Kesterson, for example—are not calculated.)

all North American waterfowl use California wetlands as a stopover or winter residence. Depauperated though it is, California's winter waterfowl habitat is still the most important in the entire world.[25]

Other Disappearing Wildlife Habitats

Too long ago for most living Americans to remember, the arid West was dotted with oasis-like marshes and shallow lakes that served as important feeding and resting places for waterfowl on their arduous migrations. As more and more water has been

---

[25] Heitmeyer, "Valleys of California."

diverted for irrigation, these natural features of the landscape have steadily disappeared or shrunk. In Utah, for example, Sevier Lake is now dry because irrigation has reduced the flow of its water source, the Sevier River, from more than 1,100,000 to just 45,000 annual acre-feet. Vast, eerily beautiful Pyramid Lake in Nevada, the terminus of the Truckee River, has seen its surface level drop by more than 40 feet, causing the extinction of the native strain of Lahonton cutthroat trout, a huge fish once found in great numbers; the cui-ui, a fish found nowhere else, is now considered endangered. The bureau's Newlands Irrigation Project is mainly responsible—as it is for the steady disappearance of nearby Carson Lake and surrounding wetlands (now the increasingly duckless Stillwater Wildlife Management Area), which teemed with migratory waterfowl before the project was begun. Similar examples are plentiful throughout the West.[26]

Where the Bureau of Reclamation has offered any mitigation at all, it is usually in the form of an interruptible, year-to-year water supply; irrigation return flows are also delivered to remnant or artificially created marshes. Lately, however, the Fish and Wildlife Service and state fish and game agencies have expressed considerable alarm about the cumulative burden of pesticides, herbicides, and concentrated mineral salts present in most used irrigation water. A recent Interior Department report warned of potentially disastrous, Kesterson-like consequences at nearly two dozen western wildlife refuges if more fresh water is not mixed into the polluted return flows.[27]

The Colorado River

The Colorado River is, to some environmentalists, an example of how the dam-builders take away and how the dam-builders give back. On the one hand, the main-stem and tributary dams (of which the Bureau of Reclamation has built over a dozen on the

---

[26] Ibid. Other chapters in Smith's book are a good source of information on extinct or vanishing wildlife habitat outside of California.

[27] See *Reconnaissance Investigation of Water Quality, Bottom Sediment, and Biota Associated with Irrigation Drainage in the Kendrick Reclamation Project Area, Wyoming, 1986–87*, and a series of related reports available from the U.S. Geologic Survey, Denver, Colorado.

Colorado system) have evened the flow of this once wildly erratic river, permitting year-round whitewater recreation. The dams, which serve as silt traps, have also improved the water quality, or at least made it less opaque; on the other hand, the relatively siltless flows and hydropower surges are cannibalizing the river's beaches, making camping more uncomfortable and difficult (and almost impossible at high water). The two great reservoirs, Powell and Mead, offer a rare, if completely artificial, recreational opportunity: peaceful, solitary boating, fishing, and sightseeing on vast cool lakes in the hottest and most arid landscape in North America.

Lake Powell drowned one of the most gorgeous river canyons on earth, one that lifted John Wesley Powell—the godfather of the federal irrigation program—to rapturous heights. Some conservationists consider the aesthetic loss of Glen Canyon to have been the most significant in conservation history—at least in river conservation history. Hundreds more miles of whitewater and wild river canyon bottoms have been drowned on the Colorado and major tributaries such as the Green and San Juan. The second most significant loss in the Colorado system has probably been that of the delta itself, at the head of the Gulf of California. A teeming refuge for waterfowl, game birds, and jaguars as late as the 1920s, when Aldo Leopold wrote glowingly of his hunting adventures there, it has virtually disappeared from thirst.[28]

Rare and Endangered Species, Recreation, and Other Environmental Matters

Riparian bottomlands are important to wildlife almost everywhere. In arid zones, however, they are extraordinarily important, because constant streams, and the vegetative cover that grows along them, may be dozens or hundreds of miles apart in a desert landscape. Humans somehow manage to forget that other animals need water just as they do. Water development, however, often causes drastic disruptions of hydrological regimes that have prevailed for millennia and on which countless gener-

---

[28] A. Leopold, *A Sand County Almanac* (Oxford University Press, 1949).

ations in a given animal population have grown dependent. In arid regions, it usually results in the formation of a large body of water—a reservoir—in one isolated location and then little or no water in the natural streambed for many miles, due to irrigation diversions. Much of the water that does manage to leach back to the river has percolated through intensively cultivated soil; it carries a heavy load of salts, toxic minerals, and agricultural chemicals. Reduced streamflows also tend to raise the thermal gradient substantially, harming sensitive species such as salmon, which tolerate temperatures higher than 68°F very poorly. (In 1987, warm water released into the American River from a drawn-down and heated Folsom Lake killed the vast majority of juvenile fish at the Nimbus hatchery near Sacramento.) There are incidences, however, where reservoirs have made rivers colder, to the benefit of both native and introduced species of fish—usually trout.[29]

Nothing suffers so much from highly regulated and depleted river flows as riparian vegetation, which depends on very high groundwater tables (in effect, the portion of the river flowing underground) and seasonal flooding for survival. Almost everywhere in the West, riparian trees, forests, marshes, and willow shrublands have declined dramatically since the federal government got into the dam-building business. (Obversely, and ironically, some greatly depleted streambeds in wetter zones, such as California's Trinity River, are being choked and narrowed by encroaching vegetation, which is no longer cleared away by floods.) More than 90 percent of the riparian woodlands in the Sacramento River floodplain—forests that once covered hundreds of square miles—are gone. As a result, the yellow-billed cuckoo, utterly dependent on large riparian trees for nesting and food, is nearly extinct, and wood ducks, once very common in California, are now quite rare.[30] On the Platte River, the problem is exactly the opposite: The greatly depleted flows through Nebraska and eastern Colorado have let shrub vegetation take over the braided river's islands and usurp migrating sandhill

---

[29] Personal communication with William Kier, California Salmon-Steelhead Advisory Committee.

[30] W. Kahrl et al., *California Water Atlas* (Department of Water Resources, 1978, 1979).

and whooping cranes, two of the stateliest (and, in the case of the whooper, rarest) waterfowl on the planet.[31]

There are some instances where water development has been a boon to fish and wildlife species. Lake Mead supports a thriving striped bass fishery—a partial replacement for the badly depleted striper fishery in California's Delta and San Francisco Bay, a casualty of Central Valley and State Water Project pumps (as well as Pacific Gas and Electric's power plants). Releases from Hetch Hetchy Reservoir, on California's famous Tuolumne River, to Don Pedro Reservoir downstream support an excellent trout fishery all year long, where the unregulated river nearly dried up in late summer and fall. The controlled, reliable flows have also been a boon for the whitewater rafting business— which is also the case on the Trinity, Rogue, South Fork American, Colorado, and other important recreational rivers in the West. (One could argue, however, that this is fair and minimal recompense for the thousands of wild river miles lost to reservoirs.) And it goes without saying that artificial lakes in an arid climate are regarded as a godsend by a great many people who are not inclined, or are physically unable, to enjoy whitewater recreation and stream fishing.

On balance, one could probably conclude that federal water development in the West has done the natural environment a lot of harm and some good. The word "natural" is often taken to mean anything not urban, but in the strictest sense it means those species of flora and fauna, and those features of the landscape, that were native and unaltered before humans arrived on the scene. Using that definition, the harm caused by water development becomes much greater. It is true that, in many cases, introduced species—striped bass, eastern brook trout, crappie—have thrived. (Most of these species, as that short list implies, are fish.) But many of the West's signature native species, some of which were once fabulously abundant, have gone into drastic decline. (We speak mainly of fauna here, though the negative impact on some flora has been profound, too. In Arizona, for example, riparian cottonwood trees have become extremely rare.) All the ducks, geese, and swans found in the West;

---

[31] National Audubon Society, *Audubon Wildlife Report 1988/1989*, p. 285.

salmon and steelhead; cranes; bald eagles; white pelicans; big-horn sheep; elk—these are species which, for the most part, have not tolerated water development well at all. Other factors may have figured prominently in their decline (particularly in the case of large land mammals), but water projects, especially for irrigation, have often played the dominant role.

For species such as ducks and salmon to recover even some-what, it is absolutely essential that more fresh water be ear-marked for them. The status quo, in other words, is not good enough, unless we do not mind seeing their numbers continue to decline. To provide *more* water for wildlife and the natural envi-ronment at the same time urban and agricultural water demand keeps rising may seem impossible. Whether that is true or not, it is surely one of the great environmental challenges for the 1990s. And one of the key roles in that effort could, and should, be played by the Bureau of Reclamation.

The "New" Bureau of Reclamation

In 1987, the Bureau of Reclamation, implying that the great dam-building era has finally come to an end, announced that it intends to overhaul its policies and redefine its mission. Subse-quently, the agency said that its new planning goals would address "the role Reclamation can play as the transition is made from the policies and practices of this century to the changing priorities and needs of the next."[32]

Is this happening? Is the bureau serious about revising poli-cies that appear to be etched in stone (or, as the case may be, concrete)? In some instances the answer is yes. But, two years later, the long-awaited transition has barely begun. This may be an opportune place to mention some new policies (announced or implemented) for which the bureau deserves credit—and, at the same time, to demonstrate how, in important ways, the bureau's mission shows no signs of changing at all.

---

[32] Bureau of Reclamation, *Implementation Plan: Update '89*, p. 1.

"By the turn of the century," a recent bureau planning document proclaims, "Reclamation will have shifted the focus of its mission from the development and construction of major projects to more efficient use of water through conservation and management." More specifically, in a ranking of thirteen program priorities, "construction" was listed fourth in 1988 but was expected to drop to eighth on the list by 1998. Water quality ("environmental restoration and enhancement"), on the other hand, was projected to move from fifth priority in 1988 to second in 1998. (The number one program priority, "operation and maintenance of facilities," is not to change in the foreseeable future.) These rankings, while too general to indicate what changes really might occur, do at least reflect an evolving self-image and view of the world.

Sometime afterward, in late 1988, the bureau finally announced its "policy on western water marketing," suggesting that it would serve as a "facilitator" for marketing proposals between willing buyers and sellers of federal water. (For a full text of the policy statement and implementing guidelines, see Appendix B.) In presenting the policy, Assistant Secretary for Water and Science James Ziglar declared: "Transfers have the potential for improving the efficiency of already developed water projects, which is a major goal of the Bureau." One Washington insider complained that the bureau's *draft* policy on transfers (in which the agency would have actively promoted water marketing) was much more forceful; but it was apparently quashed by political pressure exerted by certain western members of Congress. "Admittedly [the policy recommendations] are fairly general," responded one of the Interior officials who helped draft the statement, "but they set a tone for the future that I believe will benefit the nation from both an economic and environmental standpoint." Simply by announcing a policy that does not oppose transfers the bureau demonstrated that it is reevaluating its direction; the true test, however, will come when farmers seek to transfer water they have saved through conservation efforts.

At least a few of the bureau's recent initiatives and activities do seem to reflect some fresh thinking. For example:

- The agency's 1989 budget request proposed eleven new planning studies to increase the efficiency of existing projects, protect groundwater quality, and look into nonstructural water development and management alternatives.

- The bureau has taken an active role in addressing the ongoing western drought, establishing points of contact to coordinate drought management activities with other federal, state, and local agencies, and assisting water users with temporary water transfers or exchanges during periods of shortage.

- The bureau is experimenting with a novel method of lining earthen canals without draining them. If this technique proves feasible, 66 unlined miles of the Coachella and All-American canals may soon be improved, saving an estimated 100,000 acre-feet of water each year.

- Consistent with its announced policy of protecting and enhancing environmental values, the bureau is helping to restore fisheries in several areas across the West. The Upper Colorado region is taking the lead by joining with other federal and state agencies in a Colorado River Endangered Fishes Recovery Plan. This congressionally funded program includes stocking native and non-native species, research, and monitoring.

- The bureau is now involved in an intergovernmental effort to address salinity and drainage-related problems in California's San Joaquin Valley. Participating agencies besides the Bureau of Reclamation include the California Department of Fish and Game, California Department of Water Resources, U.S. Fish and Wildlife Service, and the U.S. Geological Survey. Various alternatives to the "Master Drain" (referred to by some as "Super Kesterson") are apparently under discussion.

A cynic might observe that these new initiatives look very much like elements of President Carter's water policy reform proposal of 1978, which was relentlessly undermined by western political interests, sometimes with tacit cooperation from the bureau itself. That aside, some of its ongoing activities remain hopelessly at odds with its supposed transformation. In particular, the bureau has refused to put its supposed new operating principles in motion in the case of several precedent-setting Central Valley Project water service contracts now up for renewal. Its inability to reconcile promise with deed has already

50

led it into a political minefield and major litigation over contracts for water delivered through the project's Friant Unit.

The Friant Unit supplies twenty-eight districts and municipalities holding water service contracts with the bureau. Under these contracts, the government delivers approximately 1.5 million acre-feet of water each year from the project's reservoirs. (Because the first contracts for water deliveries from the Friant Unit were executed in the late 1940s, all are about to expire.) In early 1989, the bureau completed the first of the renegotiations. Contrary to its announced recognition of environmental values, there was no environmental review at all—despite the fact that Friant Dam destroyed the third most important salmon run in California and most of the San Joaquin River's riparian habitat. Not only that, but the bureau promised to deliver the same amount of water for the next forty years at an inflation-adjusted price *even lower* than the original one—already hugely subsidized. No pricing alternatives, conservation possibilities, or environmental mitigation measures were even mentioned.

In January 1989, a number of senators and congressmen wrote President George Bush and Secretary of the Interior Manuel Lujan urging them not to permit any Friant Unit contract renewals without an extensive environmental review. "If even a small percentage of this water could be conserved by Friant water users," they wrote, "it would be available for other users in the CVP system, or elsewhere in California. The Interior Department's proposed actions completely ignore such possibilities."[33]

At about the same time, a coalition of twelve environmental groups, led by the Natural Resources Defense Council and the Sierra Club Legal Defense Fund, sued to enjoin the Bureau of Reclamation from signing the Friant Unit contracts. In February 1989, a federal judge issued a temporary restraining order halting the renewals; this was later modified to allow the renewals on the condition that all contract provisions would remain subject to review by the court. Litigation over the question of whether environmental review is required prior to contract

---

[33] This letter, dated January 9, 1989, was written by Senators Bill Bradley and Richard Lugar and Representatives George Miller and Thomas Petri.

51

renewal is continuing as we go to press. The outcome will be extraordinarily important: The terms of the Friant renewals are expected to set a precedent for 300 other water service contracts covering the entire length of the Central Valley—and involving 7 million acre-feet of water. It will provide a crucial test of the bureau's commitment to conservation, efficiency, and environmental protection—objectives the agency is supposed to be reconciling with its traditional goals. The real question is: Why did environmental organizations have to drag the Bureau of Reclamation into court to make it do essentially what it has been promising to do for the past two years?

One can point to other Bureau of Reclamation policies that contravene, if they do not altogether mock, its announced new mission. For example, the bureau is now trying to sell 1.5 million acre-feet of water from the Central Valley Project which it regards as "surplus"—that is, unneeded for any other purpose and available for purchase by agricultural interests. Since the California State Water Resources Control Board (SWRCB) is still trying to determine how much freshwater outflow is needed for the long-term survival of the San Francisco Bay–Delta ecosystem (a water rights decision is not expected before 1991), it seems shortsighted—to say the least—for the bureau to attempt to sell water that it may soon be ordered to release into the Bay–Delta estuary instead. (Preliminary findings and SWRCB staff reports suggest that the Bay and Delta may need several million more acre-feet of fresh water annually.) What is more, most of the state and federal wildlife refuges in California are begging for water—the voters even authorized substantial funds to purchase it in 1986—but the bureau's sole concession to California wetlands is 2,000 additional acre-feet of water earmarked for the Grasslands Wildlife Management Area. Since the habitat this minuscule amount of water can sustain is far less than the 1,200 acres of condemned wetlands at the Kesterson National Wildlife Refuge, the bureau, in this particular instance, appears to be flouting the Bush administration's stated goal of "no further net loss" of wetlands acreage across the fifty states.

Meanwhile, one cannot accuse the bureau of haste or recklessness when it comes to implementing the water use efficiency goals it announced with such fanfare in 1988. Thus far, its only real accomplishment is its announced intention to line the All-American and Coachella canals in California. Interviews with the bureau's leadership in Denver leave the impression that the agency has no plans to implement on-farm conservation strategies—although it is on the farms, not in the canals, where most agricultural water waste occurs. One could argue that this is a job for the Department of Agriculture or state water managers, but the Bureau of Reclamation is not even taking any steps to cooperate with these other agencies.

Many conservationists, and even some former top-level Interior officials, have suggested that the bureau has outlived its usefulness and ought to be ceremoniously interred—as the Synthetic Fuels Corporation was a few years ago. We have not given this question—should the bureau even continue to exist?—the careful thought it deserves, largely because its abolition would create a political, administrative, and water-rights nightmare whose solution is not our purpose here. Who would then "own" its canals and dams? What about the rights to more than 30 million acre-feet of water it provides? Who would be responsible for dam maintenance? For emergency decisions regarding drought allocations or fish-flow releases? Moreover, any attempt to abolish the Bureau of Reclamation would be fanatically resisted by many politicians and organized constituencies in the western states, precipitating a political battle that may not be justified by its results.

As we will demonstrate later, the main obstacle to the more efficient and environmentally benign use of water in the western states is not so much the Bureau of Reclamation as long-standing federal water policy and water law itself. In our view, modernizing western water law and policy is far more important than trying to dismantle a bureaucracy which, in large measure, is simply a creature of both. That is the enormous problem we address in Part II.

Water and the Law: How the West's Most Valuable Resource Is Allocated, Used, and Wasted

W H E N millions of acre-feet of water are raising crops that are in surplus, that are of extremely low value, or that grow to perfection on rainfall in a couple of dozen other states—or all of the above—then in no sense is that water being efficiently used. The same applies, we might add, to western cities—Denver, Sacramento, Fresno, and Reno are a few—where water metering is uncommon or unknown or where domestic users are charged flat monthly rates no matter how much water they consume.

We recognize that one person's "waste" can be another's necessity. Rice grown in semiarid California is very important to the economy of the Sacramento River Valley, just as cheap unmetered water is attractive to companies or families contemplating a move to Fresno. But huge, fuel-gobbling American cars were similarly important to the economy of Michigan—and even that of the United States as a whole—in 1972. By 1978, however, Detroit's outdated and grotesquely inefficient cars were a drag on the U.S. economy, and a threat to national security, that easily outweighed the benefits they offered in the form of economic activity and jobs. Through a combination of skyrocketing oil prices and mandatory fuel-efficiency standards, the U.S. auto industry was forced to confront the reality of declining petroleum production and the foreign competition this historic development spawned. And despite some very hard economic times as it tried to retool (at a cost of billions) and sell obsolete automobiles at the same time, Detroit was saved from burial by its own hand.

The water situation in the West is not exactly analogous, since water, unlike petroleum, is a renewable resource and we do not have to import it from overseas. But the inefficiency of water use in the West—particularly agricultural water use—is an increasingly important national problem that must be addressed. If it is not, this country may be forced to build more dams and sacrifice more rivers and natural beauty that, by rights, are for our children to enjoy. (The Navajo tribe has a saying about profligacy— "you are eating your grandchildren"—which, we think, applies very well here.) In simple economic terms, the cost of those dams will be exorbitant: Even allowing for inflation, compare the $49 million construction cost of Hoover Dam with the $2 billion projected cost of Auburn Dam, which would develop about 2½ percent as much water. And the longer agriculture uses 80 to 90 percent of the West's water while producing a much smaller fraction of its economic activity, the worse relations between urban and rural regions will become. (And the urban regions own the votes.) Though the West's irrigation farmers have, in the main, resisted efforts to promote more efficient water use, such a goal is eminently in their interest, too.

We need to insert one brief caveat here: Many of the problems we described in Part I clearly involve water *quality* issues, as well as questions of water allocation. Despite their close connection (Kesterson would not have occurred if farmers had not watered, or overwatered, poorly drained lands and leached excessive quantities of selenium into the return flows), water quality and water allocation seldom are addressed by the same laws, or even the same agencies. Most states monitor water quality through a health agency and deal with water allocation through a state engineer's office or natural resources department. These separate administrators seldom confer about common problems; sometimes they even adopt conflicting solutions. A few states have merged water quality and water allocation functions in a single agency—Washington's Department of Ecology is a notable example—but melding agencies is not usually enough in itself. Instead, states need to examine (and, when necessary, revise) their water codes to determine where they may protect or improve water quality by regulating water use. While there are many opportunities for improvement, our focus is on how water quality could be promoted through reallocation of existing water supplies.

The federal government, too, has a role in water quality protection, which can be quite broad and pervasive—as demonstrated by the scope of the Clean Water Act. (In contrast, the federal government routinely defers to states' decisions concerning water allocation, despite its control over much of the irrigation water delivered to the West.) We do not deal with the potential reach of this federal jurisdiction, beyond acknowledging that it is very great indeed, but we view the federal role in western water quality protection as certain to expand; too many severe pollution problems, particularly of agricultural origin, remain unaddressed. Many of our suggestions, therefore, are aimed at Congress, the present administration, and the Department of the Interior—governmental bodies that do not immediately come to mind when one thinks of western water management. As with our recommendations to the states, we urge the federal government to protect water quality by better exercising its control over water allocation (primarily through the Bureau of Reclamation). Without stronger incentives to conserve, few farmers will curtail wasteful (and polluting) irrigation practices.

From an economist's or environmentalist's point of view, the most efficient and least disruptive means of solving future water shortages in the West (and many water quality problems as well) is through what is known as water marketing, or simply water transfers. These can involve permanent sales of water rights, temporary sales of water (leases), drought-year options, and a variety of creative permutations. Thus far, water transfers have mainly involved the sale or lease of agricultural water rights to cities or industries, though one can just as easily imagine high-altitude farmers who can raise only low-value crops selling water to low-altitude irrigators raising high-value crops.

In a state such as California, with its unparalleled water supply infrastructure, water marketing could be a largely nonstructural solution to water shortages: Thousands of miles of existing canals and aqueducts can move water up, down, and across the state to wherever demand crops up. In other states with less developed infrastructures, a city, industry, or irrigation district buying water rights might have to build a pipeline to the source—as Washoe County in Nevada is planning to do, having purchased an option on groundwater in nearby Honey Lake Basin—but rarely would a new mainstream dam have to be built (although, in some instances, offstream storage reservoirs may be necessary).

The promise of more wild rivers preserved is just one of the environmental benefits of water marketing. Fallow agricultural lands can revert to native grasslands or wetlands, letting natural flora and fauna repropagate. Whether farmers sell all their water rights or just the rights to water they manage to conserve, irrigation return flows are reduced and problems with pesticides, salts, toxic minerals, and waterlogging are alleviated. (In the Colorado River Basin, according to the Bureau of Reclamation, each additional part per million of measured salinity costs urban users several hundred thousand dollars per year, due to the corrosive effect of salts on infrastructure; retiring the worst salt-plagued farmlands would not only free up a great deal of water, but would also save urban users many millions of dollars annually.)[1] Since cities consumptively use less water, per acre-foot withdrawn, than irrigated agriculture, major transfers of water to urban users could create more reliable flows for fish, wildlife, and recreation—even for downstream agriculture. Moreover, urban water is often returned to a river in a less contaminated state than if it has percolated through chemically farmed croplands—especially if they overlie thick alkaline deposits, as many western farms do.

Advocating the free market system as a cure for environmental ills is always a risky proposition; it is easy to find a thousand instances where unfettered capitalism has created environmental harm. But in the case of western water (at least for now) the transfer of water rights shows great promise as a means of achieving several important goals at once: supplying water-short urban areas *while* alleviating the drainage and salinity crisis *while* reducing surplus crop payments *while* promoting ecological health—all at a reasonable cost *without* new dams.

If all this is true—and if the West has the fastest rate of urban population growth in the nation—why isn't more water marketing going on? There is no simple answer. Most urban water managers were trained as civil engineers, and when a water shortage looms the reflex reaction of most engineers is to go out and build a dam. Some rural regions have fiercely resisted water marketing—even if individual farmers stand to make a lot of money selling or leasing water—because they view it as a prescription for their economic demise. In some cases, the necessary water delivery infrastructure does not exist. Some observers theorize that the idea is so novel that water planners have not come to terms with it yet.

Our conclusion, however, is that the most daunting obstacles to water marketing have been—and still are—made of paper. From the fundamental doctrine of appropriative rights to the bylaws of obscure irrigation districts, the corpus of western water law, procedure, policy, and custom at least inhibits water

---

[1] M. El-Ashry and D. Gibbons, *Troubled Waters: New Policies for Managing Water in the American West* (World Resources Institute, 1986).

transfers; in many instances they are prohibited outright. A few western states have gone to some lengths to revise their laws and policies so that more water transfers may occur; others have not. The Bureau of Reclamation—which delivers about a third of the surface irrigation water used in the West—has endorsed the idea in a limited sense but has done little to make it happen. And even where the law appears to permit water transfers, uncertainty as to whether it *really* does so is a major obstacle in its own right.

In this section we examine the legal obstacles to water marketing, and the reasons they exist, at some length; we survey the success of various states in modifying or removing them; and we look at some significant water transfers that have already occurred. Then, in Part III, we suggest how enlightened, carefully crafted water marketing policies could solve the West's worsening water shortage for many more years.

The Basics of Western Water Law

By now it is a truism that water played *the* crucial role in the settlement of the American West. Without water for irrigation, "reclamation" of what was once known as the Great American Desert would have been impossible. And without water to work the placers, the first western industry—mining—would not have developed at the frenzied pace that encouraged the huge western migration in the mid-1800s. Water continues to play a vital role in America's arid region today, in far more diverse and subtle ways. In many instances, for example, water is more valuable economically (not to mention aesthetically) when it is left running in a stream to support recreation and tourism than when it is diverted for industrial or agricultural uses.

In light of its pivotal role in western development, water quickly attained an exalted status as early territorial and state governments were formed. Every western state's constitution or water code provides that water is a public resource—it belongs to everyone. While these laws authorize (and indeed encourage) individuals to divert the water and put it to productive use, the

60

water itself remains the property of the public. What each di-verter "owns" is the *right to use* the water, not the water itself. Despite the implication of the term "water marketing," water is not simply a commodity to be bought, sold, and traded. As discussed in more detail later, only the legal interests in the water (appropriative water rights) may be "owned" and trans-ferred to others.

These constitutional and statutory provisions imply that all members of the public—not just the farmers and other appropriators—have a continuing interest in how water is allo-cated and managed. Theoretically, at least, we are *all* parties to a water appropriation or transfer. In an effort to protect these important interests, more and more states are enacting a variety of protective measures: special consideration for residents of river basins from which water is exported ("area of origin" protection); preservation of adequate streamflows to maintain fish and riparian vegetation ("instream flow" protection); and criteria for evaluating effects of water appropriations and trans-fers on the general welfare ("public interest" protection). All these measures are examined in the pages that follow.

If such protective measures had existed and been vigorously enforced in California when Friant Dam was constructed earlier in this century, the San Joaquin River chinook salmon run might not have gone extinct. The enormous freshwater fishery in Nevada's Pyramid Lake might not have been nearly destroyed by the federal Newlands Irrigation Project—much as Mono Lake's fishery and waterfowl rookeries have received limited protection from Los Angeles' water diversions, courtesy of the California courts. (The Mono Lake story is summarized on page 77.) On the other hand, regulatory controls intended to pro-tect broad public values can seriously impair the very water transfers that we believe would best serve the public interest and certain environmental values. Therefore, while we accept the objectives of these controls and do not argue for their elim-ination, we do suggest some legislative and administrative changes that might reduce the barriers imposed by these mea-sures.

To put it another way, the protective measures mentioned above may be viewed either as essential tools for incorporating public values into water management decisions or as annoying, expensive barriers to the efficient allocation and reallocation of water resources. In a sense, both views are correct. As we explained early on, we are advocating the increased use of market incentives to accomplish many of the same goals that currently are the subject of these state regulatory programs. Where water marketing and public protection measures clash, we hope that a balance will be struck in favor of the most equitable solution. We do not presume to know what that balance will be.

The Origins of Prior Appropriation

Nearly all western water transfers occur within the context of the prior appropriation doctrine, the primary rule governing water allocation in the West. This most fundamental of laws governing western water use did not evolve from irrigation battles, as many believe, but from the California Gold Rush. As one legal historian notes:

> The discovery of gold in the Sierra foothills of California in January 1848 and the great mining industry that followed had a profound influence, not only upon the political and economic growth of California, but upon the development of water law in this State and throughout the West. The association of gold and water came about because much of the gold was extracted from the ground by means of hydraulic or placer mining processes in which the use of water was essential. Rights to the use of water therefore became fundamentally important.[2]

Out of the customs of California miners, then, emerged the prevalent rule of western water allocation, often expressed simply as "first in time, first in right." In contrast to the riparian doctrine that developed in eastern states,[3] the prior appropriation doctrine recognizes superior rights in the first person or party to put water to use anywhere, regardless of whether the

---

[2] W. Hutchins, *The California Law of Water Rights* (Sacramento, 1956), p. 41.

[3] Riparian rights allow the owners of land adjacent to a water source to divert water for use on lands within the original watershed. Water rights held under the riparian doctrine typically may not be transferred to others for use on nonadjacent lands. Those without streamside acreage may effectively be left high and dry.

irrigated land is contiguous to a stream. Western water law is based fundamentally on water use, rather than landownership.

Today, nine western states follow the "pure" prior appropriation doctrine: Alaska, Arizona, Colorado, Idaho, Montana, Nevada, New Mexico, Utah, and Wyoming. Nine others (California, Oregon, Texas, Washington, Kansas, Nebraska, North Dakota, South Dakota, and Oklahoma) have adopted prior appropriation but have also retained riparian rights to some extent.[4] All except Colorado now require appropriators to obtain permits before water may be diverted, but otherwise the basic elements of the prior appropriation doctrine remain remarkably similar to those developed in the late 1800s.

An appropriative water right becomes vested when a person intentionally diverts water and applies it to a beneficial use. State water codes require various procedural steps, such as giving public notice and obtaining a permit from an administrative agency. What constitutes a "beneficial use" is defined more specifically in some states than others,[5] but the requirement does not differentiate between more economically or socially useful purposes. The key to establishing a water right is to prove one's priority date. Unlike stream administration in riparian systems (where the burden of water shortages is shared among users), senior appropriators receive their entire entitlement so long as there is enough water flowing in the stream for them; junior appropriators may get nothing in a dry year. (Thus, first in time, first in right.)

Another tenet of prior appropriation law is the "use it or lose it" rule. Once established according to state requirements, an appropriative water right continues to exist as long as the water is beneficially used. A right may be deemed "abandoned" if the appropriator intentionally discontinues use for several years. On the other hand, water rights are "forfeited" if not used for a period of time established by statute, regardless of the appropriator's intentions. Water lost through abandonment or forfei-

---

[4] D. Getches, *Water Law in a Nutshell* (West Publishing Co., 1984), p. 6.

[5] Traditional, utilitarian applications of water have always been included in the statutory definition: irrigation, livestock watering, industrial, and domestic uses. More recently state legislatures have included recreational uses and fish and wildlife habitat protection. See, for example, Colo. Rev. Stat. §37-92-102(3).

ture reverts to the stream for use by other appropriators. State administrators may apply these rules to curtail excessive appropriations ("paper rights" exceeding any reasonable application of water to beneficial use). At the same time, such rules may provide a disincentive to conservation: Water salvaged through improved irrigation—until transferred to another user—is subject to loss through the literal language of most states' abandonment/forfeiture rules. This problem could be solved fairly easily through statutory revision, but few states have taken this important step. (See the discussion of salvage laws on pages 78–79.)

Despite the logical (and often hydrogeological) connection between surface water and groundwater, most states do not administer the two types of water through the same allocation system. Ignoring the common-pool nature of the resource, a few states declare that a landowner overlying an aquifer is the absolute owner of all the groundwater under the property. (Texas is the only *western* state with this doctrine.) Most others have modified this concept by requiring that a pumper's withdrawals be "reasonable." Colorado has comprehensively integrated management of surface water and tributary groundwater—a practical recognition of the relationship of these two water sources. Most states require a pumper to obtain a well-drilling permit for larger extractions, but few have any comprehensive regulatory scheme to control groundwater withdrawal. Arizona, with its 1980 Groundwater Management Act, has the strictest groundwater controls. Several other states have enacted "critical area" legislation in attempts to alleviate groundwater "mining," or use far in excess of natural replenishment.

Problems with the Prior Appropriation System

The rationale of the prior appropriation system is to protect the expectations of those who invest in water diversions from interference by those who enter the picture later. A junior may not move in upstream and divert water if the diversion will compromise a senior's right. This system made sense to the early miners (especially the earliest) who laid similar claims to their gold diggings, as well as to early irrigators who staked everything on a reliable source of water for their crops. It makes sense today to cities holding old water rights or those with enough money to purchase turn-of-the-century rights from farmers.

The prior appropriation doctrine, in other words, evolved in response to the unique conditions and needs of the American West in the mid-1800s. It reflects the need for certainty in establishing water rights. It does *not* reflect concern that water be allocated equitably, as new conditions develop. Some have suggested that with America's changing values and expectations for public resources, the doctrine no longer provides the best means of allocating water. Indeed, with most of the western rivers fully appropriated (or even overappropriated, as in the case of the Colorado River), we hardly need laws encouraging new diversions. What we really need is an equitable system of reallocating existing water rights—one that implicitly shows greater concern for community values, our children's future, and our degraded environment. Some have argued—quite persuasively, at times—that the prior appropriation doctrine should be scrapped altogether and replaced with another allocation scheme, maybe even a modified version of the eastern riparian rights doctrine, which provides for shared reductions in times of drought.

We will not examine this proposition further because in our view the prior appropriation doctrine is so firmly entrenched in western laws and customs that its abolition is almost unthinkable. Nonetheless, we will not hesitate to suggest changes in western water codes and administrative programs. Our recommendations are not necessarily original. Several years ago, in fact, the Western Governors' Association itself published an influential report which examined how the West might increase its water use efficiency.[6] It defined efficiency in a very ambitious sense: how the West can "derive the most value from its water resources and can meet its water needs at the least cost to westerners." (Importantly, this use of the term "efficiency" does not mean "engineering efficiency," which simply compares the amount of water applied with the amount of water consumed by

---

[6] B. Driver, *Western Water: Tuning the System* (Western Governors' Association, 1986). This report was followed by a study prepared by the WGA Water Efficiency Working Group, *Water Efficiency: Opportunities for Action* (1987). We highly recommend these two reports.

a particular use; instead, the term implies "economic" or "allocative" efficiency, which examines the values that our society places on using scarce resources.)

Water marketing can be a powerful tool for achieving this efficiency goal, concluded the report's author, Bruce Driver, "because it is voluntary, is flexible, generates much of its own data and automatically communicates the value of alternative uses." He went on to suggest a number of legal and administrative changes that states could implement to encourage water marketing. We agree with many of these suggestions and regard them as a constructive response to the charge that the prior appropriation doctrine has outlived its usefulness: If we are stuck with the system, let's make it work better.

It is entirely possible that improving the prior appropriation doctrine will not even require new statutes or regulations. Existing laws already provide important (though, for the most part, unexplored) avenues for reducing wasteful water uses. For example, the prior appropriation doctrine requires that every appropriation be for a "beneficial use." For the most part, this requirement has been applied loosely, if at all, despite its implication that wasteful applications of water are not authorized. (In fact, as we discuss on page 78, the rule has been applied in such a way as to *discourage* water conservation and salvage.) Other statutory or constitutional language may be applied to encourage efficiency, as well. Some states, such as California, require that all water uses be "reasonable." The reasonable-use definition has proved to be a more powerful tool than the beneficial-use requirement and was the basis for the State Water Resource Control Board's Decision 1600—a determination that the Imperial Irrigation District's failure to implement a water conservation plan was unlawfully wasteful. The Water Board's decision threatened the IID with losing a portion of its appropriation and prompted the much-publicized MWD/IID agreement, which we describe in Appendix A.

Greater water-use efficiency, in other words, may well be achievable through strict enforcement of existing laws. Apart from this effort, individual appropriators participating in water markets can help move water to its highest-valued uses. Water

66

rights transfers, however, are subject to a great many restrictions, the most important of which we address here.

Water Transfers in the System

Just as the prior appropriation doctrine protects the legal status quo in a watershed when new water rights are established, the system also restricts changes in water rights in order to prevent conflict between diverters. Water rights are considered "changed" when a diverter takes the water from a different point on the stream, applies the water for a different use or in a different location, or changes the season of use. Colorado statutes define at least eleven changes that require administrative approval; other states are somewhat less specific.

Why such a concern with changed water rights? Again, the law has evolved mainly to protect the legal status quo. Appropriators who invested in diversion projects on the basis of the stream conditions—the seasonal rhythms of streamflows, the return flows of those already using water upstream—want things to remain the way they were when they arrived. The right to protect these expectations belongs to every water user, so even a newcomer can object to a senior appropriator's change in the way the stream is "operated." Thus when a junior establishes a water right, the regimen of diversions and returns becomes locked in as part of the stream conditions upon which the junior is entitled to depend. A senior wishing to make a change must ensure that no downstream juniors will be harmed. In other words, the senior may not enlarge the water right by making any changes that will alter historical patterns of use in a way that harms any other appropriator. This concept is known as the "no harm" (or "no injury") rule.

While the no-harm rule provides necessary protection for subsequent appropriators, it can operate as a significant barrier to water transfers. For one thing, most prior appropriation rights are quantified on the basis of *flow* in cubic feet per second—not *volume* in acre-feet—so a water right holder does not know how much water is his to sell. Moreover, proving the quantity of one's transferable right can be extremely expensive, since both sides usually employ expert witnesses to testify on the historical consumptive use. And some states' water codes so vaguely define "injury" that almost any junior appropriator who may be affected by a transfer (no matter how slightly) can block the change, at least temporarily.

How might this obstructive rule be improved? In several ways. State water codes might be amended, for instance, to include specific standards for what constitutes "injury" to a junior appropriator. The statutes might be revised to protect juniors against *substantial* injury—allowing transfers to go forward if the impact on others is only minimal. Similarly, an injured junior might be required to accept a substitute water source of equal quality or a modification of his diversion, provided at the expense of the party seeking to effect a water transfer.[7]

Water Transfer Procedures

Each state has its own procedures for reviewing proposed water transfers, but all contain certain common elements. Typically, a water rights holder initiates a transfer by submitting an application for a change to the administrative agency with jurisdiction over water resources. The agency may choose to alter the application so that it conforms to official records; then the application is filed and a fee is paid. State fees range from $5 to $150, and applicants usually must pay the costs of public notice as well. At this point objecting parties (usually junior water rights holders) may protest the change by filing objections. Disputed applications are resolved in formal hearings—usually before an administrative agency, though Colorado has a whole layer of judicial arbitration known as the water courts. In most cases, agency decisions may be appealed to a court.[8]

Depending on which state's laws are applied and on the de-

---

[7] These proposals were explained in D. O'Brien, "Water Marketing in California," *Pacific Law Journal*, vol. 19 (1988):1165. We reiterate them, along with other recommended changes in the no-harm rule, in Part III.

[8] For specific elements of western states' transfer procedures see B. Colby and M. McGinnis, *Water Transfer Procedures and Transactions Costs in Eight Western States* (draft, University of Arizona, 1988).

gree of opposition to the change, this whole procedure may take a month or may last over a year.[9] Colorado—noted for its early acceptance of the *idea* of transfers—is notorious for freighting the "right of free transferability" with the West's most time-consuming and expensive process, which one economist described as "a needlessly costly and uncertain system in which innovation is difficult."[10] Despite these inconveniences, Colorado water is actively traded within water conservation districts. Districts using "developed" water (imported from a different watershed) are not subject to legal restrictions aimed at protecting return flows and thus are free to change water uses freely within their boundaries. (Relatively free trading among farmers *within* water service districts is common in other western states, too, including California.)

Some states have taken measures to reduce transfer costs and delays. In New Mexico, for example, the state engineer determines transferable water quantities by applying formulas based on crop type and irrigation method. Protests must be filed within ten days after notice of the application is filed, and the state engineer encourages parties to resolve their differences privately.[11] Similarly, transfer proceedings may be simplified if a state provides for less formal procedures in cases where there are no significant objections from third parties fearing injury from someone else's sale or lease of water rights. Nevada gives an objector the choice of making a formal or informal protest. Nevada law also provides for a novel, very western approach to conflict resolution: a field investigation in which the arguing parties are gathered at the site of the old or proposed new water use (often without their attorneys) to present their positions to the agency staff.[12] Although such alternative approaches can be efficient and should be encouraged, more formal procedures

---

[9] For a summary of water transfers in western states from 1963 to 1982 see R. Higginson and J. Barnett, *Water Rights and Their Transfer in the Western United States* (Conservation Foundation, 1984), table 3.

[10] T. Tregarthen, "Water in Colorado: Fear and Loathing in the Marketplace," in *Water Rights: Scarce Resource Allocation, Bureaucracy and the Environment*, ed. R. Anderson (Pacific Institute for Public Policy Research, 1983), pp. 119–136.

[11] For a description of the dispute resolution process in New Mexico see Colby and McGinnis, *Water Transfer*, pp. 13–17.

[12] Ibid., p. 26.

must be available to resolve protests when informal methods do not work.

In summary, then, the no-harm rule provides the fundamental protection demanded by other water users who might be affected by a senior appropriator's decision to transfer a water entitlement. But that leaves out many other interests—residents in a river basin from which water will be exported, fish and wildlife dependent on continuing streamflows, and others whose interests simply were not addressed by frontier lawmakers in the nineteenth century. In the next section we examine how western states have begun to recognize and protect such diverse interests.

State Laws and Policies

All seventeen western states base their water codes on the doctrine of appropriative rights, and that doctrine's fundamental tenets—"first in time, first in right" and "use it or lose it"—are applied in essentially the same manner. Over the decades, however, various states have amended their water codes in order to deal rationally and equitably (at least as they see it) with certain problems that have arisen during the application of appropriative rights doctrine. While all the western state water codes are similar at heart, they do differ in some important respects, and these permutations may affect water transfer negotiations—sometimes profoundly. In this section, we elaborate on a few of them.

Area of Origin Protection

By effectively detaching the West's water from the land, the prior appropriation doctrine fundamentally favors movement of water from one river basin to another. Indeed, such "transbasin diversions" are often necessary in order to move water from streams to irrigable farmland. The Colorado Supreme Court, in a seminal prior appropriation case, stated that "it would be an ungenerous and inequitable rule that would deprive one of its benefit simply because he has, by large expenditure of time and money, carried the water from one stream over an intervening watershed and cultivated land in the valley of another."[13] This rule represents one of the main differences between prior appropriation and the riparian doctrine that developed in humid eastern states.[14]

Transbasin diversions typically cause concern among people living in the river basins from which the water is exported (areas of origin), who fear adverse environmental, economic, and social consequences. Many of these concerns are based on real harm suffered as a result of poorly planned transfers in the past—although some have been magnified into gothic horrors that no longer reflect modern reality. The tragic fate of the Owens Valley, for example, continues to haunt rural California seventy years after Los Angeles acquired its water rights by perfectly legal subterfuge. This burdensome legacy has greatly hampered that state's efforts to implement water marketing, even though much stronger protections now exist against a recurrence of an "Owens Valley episode."[15]

In response to such concerns, some western states have enacted what are generically known as "area of origin" statutes. They include: (1) prohibitions against or severe restrictions on transbasin diversions; (2) reservation of water or preferences for those living in areas of origin; and (3) compensation for harm suffered by the export basins.[16] Few western states have followed the first approach and erected barriers to transbasin diversions (prohibitions are common in riparian rights jurisdictions); Arizona and Montana, however, have enacted fairly restrictive laws concerning transbasin diversions of surface water. California exemplifies the second approach, in which the basins

---

[13] *Coffin v. Left Hand Ditch Co.*, 6 Colo. 443, 449 (1882).

[14] The riparian doctrine gives owners of land near streams or lakes the right to use water on these adjacent ("riparian") lands, regardless of when the landowners entered the picture.

[15] See Reisner, *Cadillac Desert*, chap. 2, for an account of the Owens Valley water battle.

[16] This classification was developed and explained in L. MacDonnell, C. Howe, J. Corbridge, and W. Ahrens, *Guidelines for Developing Area-of-Origin Compensation* (research report, Natural Resources Law Center, University of Colorado School of Law, December 1985).

of origin are guaranteed the right to get their water back from an exporter if it is ever needed in the county in which it originates. Some have questioned the effectiveness of this approach in the long run. "Does anyone really believe," asks David Getches, one of the leading experts in water law, "that once the City of Los Angeles becomes dependent on water exported from a rural area, the rural area will be able to command return of the water because it 'needs' it?"[17] Colorado has attempted to implement the third approach with a compensation scheme in which certain transfers of water out of the Colorado River Basin must be preceded by construction of reservoirs on the Western Slope. But this approach has been criticized, too: Many of the "compensatory storage" reservoirs sit virtually unused and are not located near areas that are likely to experience much future growth.

Despite their shortcomings, such statutory protections will continue to constrain water transfers to varying degrees in all the western states. Few would argue for their elimination; the question is how areas of origin might be protected more effectively and with less burden on beneficial transfers. One suggestion is to establish a "basin equity fund" into which a person proposing to export water must deposit a fee based on the quantity of water diverted. This money could be used in a variety of ways by the area of origin to offset adverse effects of the water transfer, just as severance taxes are imposed for minerals extraction.[18]

Area of origin concerns are not restricted to moving water across watershed dividers. Water transferred from agricultural use to municipal use, even though it might remain in the same watershed, can have significant social and economic impacts. For example, a farm implement distributor or grain elevator operator might go out of business if a number of farmers in the community decide to retire and sell their water rights to a nearby growing municipality. Unlike the case of transbasin diversions, however, there are few statutory or administrative sources of protection for these "in-basin" areas of origin. This is one reason why the farm lobby in California has, for the most

---

[17] D. Getches, *Draining the Basin: What Protection Is There for an Area Whose Water Is Exported?* (Santa Fe, N.M.: Designwrights Collaborative, undated).

[18] Ibid. This option was also addressed in MacDonnell et al., *Guidelines*.

part, adamantly resisted efforts by individual farmers to sell portions of their water entitlements to nonagricultural users. Until these concerns are addressed, rural interests are unlikely to unite in supporting large-scale water transfers for municipal needs.[19]

Area of origin consequences are being addressed, and in some cases "solved," through negotiated settlements and creative sales agreements in, among other places, the Arkansas River Valley in southeastern Colorado. The cities of Aurora and Colorado Springs, both projecting rapid population growth, have acquired large blocks of water rights from farmers in that basin. In response to concerns by other water users, the cities have agreed to maintain minimum streamflows and to reseed the retired farmland with native grasses so that it may be used for raising forage and cattle (and to prevent dust-bowl conditions).[20]

Instream Flow Protection

The traditional elements of an appropriative water right include *diversion* of the water for application to a *beneficial use*. When water law was primarily a means of allocating water between miners, the diversion element served to give notice of one's right: If water remained in the stream, one could assume that it was available for appropriation. Additionally, early state lawmakers did not consider water flowing in its natural channel (instream flow) to be a beneficial use—our utilitarian predecessors thought such flows were "wasting" to the sea. In the many years that have passed since then, however, western states have come, amidst substantial conflict, to recognize the environmental, aesthetic, and even economic benefits of natural stream

---

[19] At least on balance, such fears may be exaggerated. One economist concluded that "indirect losses to a region giving up irrigation water, while not insignificant in terms of either monetary flows or employment, will be dwarfed by the gains in the non-agricultural sectors." See R. Young, *Economic Impacts of Transferring Water from Agriculture to Alternative Uses in Colorado* (Colorado Water Resources Institute Completion Report no. 122, 1983), p. 33. This does not, of course, allay the fears of the individual, whose losses may be very real indeed.

[20] "Colorado's Front Range Cities and the Arkansas Valley: What Happens When the Water Is Gone?," *Water Market Update* (February 1987):9–10.

flows. As a result, many western states' water codes have been amended to include fish and wildlife enhancement as beneficial uses of water. In addition to these statutory amendments, most western states have recently enacted instream flow protection programs, which may encourage innovative water transfers in the future. (Transfers that contradict a state's instream flow objectives presumably will be discouraged.)

Instream flow protection strategies vary tremendously between states; their effectiveness varies greatly, too. In Colorado, for example, the state Water Conservation Board (CWCB) appropriates water in order to maintain minimum streamflow and lake levels. These CWCB rights are ranked along with the rights of farmers, cities, and others. But because the program is only fifteen years old, instream flow rights tend to be quite junior in priority. Thus they offer little protection in heavily appropriated streams. The state can also purchase senior water rights and dedicate them for instream flows, a method which is much more effective but too expensive for the state to use itself. Others (the Nature Conservancy in particular) have purchased such senior rights and donated them to the state for instream flow protection. Other states (Oregon and Washington, for example) have adopted regulations establishing minimum streamflows for each basin—effectively giving top priority to the river itself. Others, such as California, have attached conditions to new permits requiring streamflow maintenance at critical periods (for example, while salmon are spawning). The state of Montana, like Colorado, authorizes government agencies to reserve unappropriated waters for instream uses, including recreation, fish and wildlife habitat, and water quality maintenance. Most of the state's reservations to date have occurred in the Yellowstone River Basin.

These state programs are all part of an important trend recognizing the diverse values of water remaining in the streambed. Most, however, do not allow private parties to hold instream flow rights. (Alaska is the only western state that legislatively authorizes privately held instream flow rights, though Arizona has recognized such rights in administrative actions.) This policy prevents individuals and organizations from actively protecting streamflow levels through participation in water markets.

It is true that organizations such as the Nature Conservancy have begun to purchase senior water rights and dedicate them to a state agency as instream flow rights. But private parties with a financial stake in flowing water—fish hatchery operators, whitewater rafting companies—have had a great deal of difficulty establishing valid instream flow appropriations. If more states allowed private parties to hold such rights, some believe that water transfer activities would increase and water allocation would more accurately reflect America's environmental, aesthetic, and economic values.

Those who oppose the private acquisition of instream flow rights claim that only a public agency will properly weigh the social benefits of instream versus out-of-stream uses and ensure consistent application of state policy. They express concern that private citizens will "lock up" the state's water by filing for unreasonably large instream appropriations. Others have argued persuasively for an intermediate approach. Many other entities (the federal government, municipalities, and other state agencies) have legitimate claims to instream flows, yet these bodies are seen as less of a threat than private instream flow appropriators.[21] The Nevada Supreme Court followed this reasoning in a recent decision recognizing federal rights to appropriate water for fishery, wildlife, and stock watering purposes on public lands in the state.[22]

Even in states lacking formal instream flow programs, private conservationists are pursuing their instream flow objectives in new, creative ways. In northern New Mexico, for example, recreational users and reservoir owners recently reached an accord for water flows in the Rio Chama. Under the terms of the agreement, more water is released on summer weekends when the river is heavily used by boaters in order to create more favorable rafting flows. The released water is captured for later use by the original owners in a downstream reservoir, so the arrangement costs them nothing. Even when no reservoir storage is available, conservationists may be able to protect instream flows by nego-

---

[21] C. Meyer, "Should the Acquisition of Instream Flow Rights Be Limited to the CWCB?" (paper presented to the Water and Environmental Law Sections, Colorado Bar Association, Colorado Springs, 1987).

[22] *Nevada v. Morros* (No. 18105, December 21, 1988).

tiating arrangements with senior appropriators to reduce diversions at critical streamflow periods or to move a point of diversion downstream. These creative measures *alone* are not enough, however, as they do not prevent other appropriators from taking advantage of the "new" water in the stream and diverting it for their purposes.

Public Interest and Public Trust Issues

Most state water codes contain a requirement that an appropriation be "consistent with the public interest," though the term, or concept, is seldom statutorily defined. This requirement has recently been interpreted as a source of protection for previously ignored interests of those who have no water rights (so-called third parties), including communities with traditional cultures[23] and fish and wildlife.[24]

The increasing application of public interest criteria to proposed water appropriations or transfers has met with a great deal of criticism. In particular, some feel that the balancing of social, economic, and environmental values is a job for elected officials, not judges or administrators:

> If such broad social decisions are to be made, they should be made by a representative body with a relatively broad-based constituency, perhaps even the state legislature. This does not mean that each water transfer decision must be reviewed and approved by some broadly representative body. It does mean that such a body should establish general criteria or plans to guide water officials in such decision making.[25]

Others have suggested that state agencies (rather than legisla-

---

[23] For example, *In the Matter of Howard Sleeper*, Rio Arriba County Cause No. RA 84-53(C) (N.M. 1st Jud. Dist., April 16, 1985), held that a proposed transfer of water from agricultural use to ski area use would adversely affect the traditions and culture of the region and therefore was contrary to the public interest. This case was reversed on appeal but received a great deal of attention nonetheless.

[24] For example, *Stempel v. Department of Water Resources*, 82 Wash. 2d 109, 508 P. 2d 166 (1973): Department of Ecology must "consider the total environmental and ecological factors to the fullest" in making its public welfare determination.

[25] G. Gould, "Water Rights Transfers and Third-Party Effects," *Land and Water Law Review*, vol. 23 (1988):1, 34.

tures) possess the experience and expertise to develop public interest standards, but they conclude that these criteria must be established as part of a comprehensive planning process, rather than as the result of ad hoc decisions.[26]

Environmental effects of water transfers may also be considered when the public trust doctrine is applied, as directed by the California Supreme Court in its 1983 Mono Lake decision.[27] In that case, the court reviewed forty-year-old water rights held by the city of Los Angeles in waters flowing into Mono Lake, a large saline lake supporting vast numbers of nesting and migratory birds with its brine fly and shrimp populations. The city's diversions were lowering the lake's level about a foot per year, affecting the saline balance and exposing the birds to increased predation as receding waters converted islands to peninsulas. Although the state had approved these rights long ago, the court concluded that the public trust imposed an affirmative duty of continuing supervision over water use: "In exercising its sovereign power to allocate water resources in the public interest, the state is not confined by past allocation decisions which may be incorrect in light of current knowledge or inconsistent with current needs."[28] One scholar recently suggested that the public trust doctrine provides an important guarantee of water quality.[29]

The growth of public interest considerations, accompanied by development of the judicial public trust doctrine, clearly do pose obstacles to the agriculture-to-urban water transfers that we propose. On the other hand, they also provide what many see as the missing link in water marketing: consideration of those who do not participate directly in water transactions. If public interests are adequately addressed when transfers are approved (for example, if areas of origin are compensated adequately),

---

[26] See, for example, D. Getches, "Water Planning: Untapped Opportunity for the Western States," *Journal of Energy Law and Policy*, vol. 9 (1988):1.

[27] *National Audubon Society v. Superior Court of Alpine County*, 33 Cal. 3d 419, 658 P.2d 709, 189 Cal. Rptr. 346, *cert. denied*, 464 U.S. 977 (1983).

[28] 189 Cal. Rptr. at 365.

[29] R. Johnson, "The Emerging Recognition of a Public Interest in Water: Water Quality Control by the Public Trust Doctrine," in *Water and the American West*, ed. D. Getches (Natural Resources Law Center, University of Colorado School of Law, 1988).

then these costs will no longer constitute externalities. This should alleviate many of the rural and environmental objections to transfers of water from agriculture to municipalities. But for now, the evolution of public trust doctrine should be considered in its infancy.

Salvaged Water

In recent years cities searching for nearby water for growing populations have proposed paying farmers to line their ditches and to install water-saving irrigation devices; in return, the cities receive the conserved (salvaged) water. The city of Casper, Wyoming, for example, obtained water by just such an arrangement with the Casper-Alcova Irrigation District. In return for rehabilitating and lining parts of the district's canal and lateral systems to reduce seepage, the city received an additional water supply of 7,000 acre-feet per year from the North Platte River.[30] Through this type of arrangement less water is consumed by agricultural use but farming is not curtailed.

At present, however, state laws pose severe obstacles to such innovative arrangements.[31] The prior appropriation doctrine mandates that water be applied to a "beneficial use" or it is no longer considered appropriated. According to traditional water law doctrine, a farmer using water for irrigation is entitled to the quantity of water *reasonably* needed for the crops being grown. If the farmer is applying excess (unreasonable) amounts of water, this water is technically not part of the appropriative right. Thus if a farmer installs water-saving technology and reduces his water use, the excess water becomes available for other appropriators to use. Never having belonged to the farmer, it is not available for sale or transfer.

This particular tenet of western water law doctrine is proba-

---

[30] R. Wahl and F. Osterhoudt, "Voluntary Transfers of Water in the West," in U.S. Geological Survey, *National Water Summary 1985*, p. 113.

[31] For a review of state policies on sale of salvaged water see G. Weatherford, ed., *Water and Agriculture in the Western U.S.: Conservation, Reallocation and Markets* (Westview Press, 1982), pp. 215–223.

bly the single greatest disincentive to innovative water conservation and transfer arrangements, and it has been the subject of increasing criticism.[32] California, Oregon, and Montana recently passed statutes allowing appropriators to retain control over waters salvaged through conservation efforts, but most western states have not taken this critically important step. Efficient water transfers and reallocation will be greatly hampered in states that continue to embrace the traditional, restrictive rule.

Not everyone agrees that salvaged water should be available for transfers. Opponents have pointed out that "wasted" water applied in excess of crop demands returns to the stream or to a groundwater basin for reuse (by riparian vegetation as well as by downstream appropriators). These return flows may serve an important hydrological regulating function by delaying streamflow; other appropriators often rely on delayed flows to supply their needs during dry summer months. Most objections, however, can be refuted or addressed by careful legislative drafting. First, although irrigation return flows may help maintain streamflows, they often are so contaminated with harsh salts, pesticides, fertilizers, and other harmful substances that they do at least as much harm as good. Second, environmental values can be protected by limiting the quantity of salvaged water that can be transferred. Oregon, for example, generally requires that 25 percent of the conserved water be reserved for instream flow enhancement; the remaining 75 percent is available for transfer. Furthermore, the state protects downstream users from deprivation by defining "conserved water" as "the amount of water, previously *unavailable to subsequent appropriators*, that results from conservation measures."[33] Thus other appropriators are protected from harm and environmental values are enhanced, while less water is applied for consumptive use by irrigated crops.

---

[32] See, for example, M. Gheleta, "Water Use Efficiency and Appropriation in Colorado: Salvaging Incentives for Maximum Beneficial Use," *University of Colorado Law Review*, vol. 58 (1988):657; A. Tarlock, "The Changing Meaning of Water Conservation in the West," *Nebraska Law Review*, vol. 66 (1987):145, 158.

[33] Or. Admin. Rules §690-18-020 (emphasis added).

Interstate Transfer Restrictions

In the past, states have attempted to preserve their water supplies by unilaterally restricting interstate water exports by statute. In 1982, however, in the *Sporhase* decision, the United States Supreme Court ruled that water is an article of interstate commerce; thus a state may not prohibit its export altogether.[34] The court did not preclude all state export controls (indeed, some states now limit exports lawfully through compacts with other states), but it required that state residents share the burden of any restrictions: "Obviously, a State that imposes severe withdrawal and use restrictions on its own citizens is not discriminating against interstate commerce when it seeks to prevent the uncontrolled transfer of water out of the State."[35] In other words, constitutionally valid state regulations affecting interstate commerce must be based on health and welfare considerations, not mere economic protectionism.

The *Sporhase* decision and its progeny[36] signal increasing judicial acceptance of water market transactions. While states may restrict transfers for valid environmental or social reasons, they may not simply ban the sale of water across state lines outright. *Sporhase* further indicates potentially vast (but currently unexercised) federal power over water resources for the purpose of conservation and efficient allocation:

> [Despite the obvious desirability of state and local control over water resources] the States' interests clearly have an interstate dimension. Although water is indeed essential for human survival, studies indicate that over 80% of our water supplies is used for agricultural purposes. The agricultural markets supplied by irrigated farms are worldwide. They provide the archetypical example of commerce among the several States for which the Framers of our Constitution intended to authorize federal regulation. The multistate character of the Ogallala aquifer [which was the source of the water at issue in

---

[34] *Sporhase v. Nebraska ex rel. Douglas*, 458 U.S. 941 (1982).

[35] 458 U.S. at 956–957.

[36] See *El Paso v. Reynolds*, 597 F. Supp. 694 (D.N.M. 1984), holding that a state may not require interstate commerce to shoulder the entire burden of furthering conservation.

this case] . . . confirms the view that there is a significant federal interest in conservation as well as in fair allocation of this diminishing resource.[37]

In essence, this language means that Congress could either facilitate or restrict water transfers in furtherance of its "conservation/allocation" authority. That is why states fearing pervasive interference in the realm of water management—traditionally the exclusive province of the states—should seize the initiative and encourage more efficient uses of water by implementing some of the changes we discuss here. Because each state's situation is unique, not every policy change is appropriate for every state. But western states might well consider how such measures might be adapted to their specific legal and political realities in order to avoid the federal preemption so many westerners fear.

Federal Water

Suppose a farmer receiving water from a Bureau of Reclamation project wants to sell or lease water rights to someone else. What, if anything, is there to sell? What is the nature of the water right? What legal barriers will hamper the attempted transfer?

The nature of a reclamation water right is not clear, even today, and the barriers to transfers appear formidable. The Department of the Interior only recently came out cautiously in favor of reclamation water transfers,[38] and the agency's hesitancy is contagious. Investors, frightened of unforeseen transaction costs and the uncertain legal status of transferred bureau water, seem to feel more secure purchasing privately appropriated water rights, even at prices several times higher than subsidized project water. Cities seeking water for growing urban

---

[37] 458 U.S. at 954.

[38] U.S. Department of the Interior, *Principles Governing Voluntary Water Transactions That Involve or Affect Facilities Owned or Operated by the Department of the Interior* (December 16, 1988). This new policy statement appears as Appendix B at the end of the book.

populations are willing to spend vast sums on new dams and pipelines when the water they need is theoretically available almost in their backyards. And farmers, unsure of the scope of their legal right to the reclamation water they receive, continue to overwater their fields with as much project water as they can get, rather than install conservation technology and sell the water they no longer need to cities.

This section attempts to resolve some of the legal questions about transferability of reclamation water. We first examine the fragmented nature of the reclamation water right and the resulting confusion over who controls the water. After reviewing real and perceived obstacles to voluntary water transfers, we suggest legislative and administrative changes to facilitate more efficient allocation.

The Reclamation Water Right

Each reclamation water right begins with an appropriation of water initiated much like any other, under prevailing state water code requirements. From that point on, however, the law regarding reclamation water little resembles that of state water rights; from a lawyer's point of view, it is more like contract law than water law. In fact, there is seldom a single reclamation "right," but rather a series of partial interests along the water distribution chain. At least initially, the Bureau of Reclamation holds the legal title (the appropriative water right). The bureau in turn enters into a service agreement with a delivery entity, such as a special water district or an irrigation district; in fact, it sometimes turns its legal title over to the district. Where the plumbing infrastructure is vast and complex, as in California's Central Valley Project, there can be successive delivery entities, each with some claim to the water originally diverted by the bureau. Finally, the irrigators who receive reclamation water own equitable title to the water right and thus are entitled to continued delivery by the federal government throughout the duration of their contracts.

Reclamation water rights are fundamentally different from privately acquired appropriative rights in one important sense: All water users within a reclamation district share the effects of drought. Thus even the most "senior" irrigator in a water district may have to reduce water usage by the same percentage as every other user in the district. Sometimes the burden is shared unequally, and deliberately so. In California's San Joaquin Valley, for example, most water districts allocate surface water on the basis of acreage served, and many give preference to lands growing permanent crops.[39] Proportional reductions and preferences appear to fly in the face of the prior appropriation doctrine's veneration of priority; they more closely resemble the method by which water is allocated during dry years in eastern states applying the riparian rights doctrine.

Despite these differences from privately held appropriative water rights, each reclamation right is fundamentally a state-granted water right; thus the states play an important auxiliary role in the bureau's decision-making. A reclamation right is created when the federal government appropriates water for a project, in conformance with all state administrative procedures for initiating an appropriation. Section 8 of the 1902 Reclamation Act[40] indicates that state law is to be considered when implementing the act, but it does not explain how state and federal interests should be balanced. Early cases tended to hold that the federal government need not comply with state laws that were inconsistent with purposes of the federal reclamation program; federal law was seen as broadly overriding state jurisdiction. In 1978, however, in a case that pitted California's stricter environmental regulations against a tradition-bound federal project, the Supreme Court construed Section 8 in a light more favorable to the states.

The case, *California v. United States,* arose when the Bureau of Reclamation applied to the California State Water Resources Control Board for a permit to appropriate water that would be impounded by the New Melones Dam, a unit of the Central Valley Project. After lengthy hearings, the board approved the bureau's application but attached twenty-five conditions to the permit, which the board concluded were necessary to meet California's statutory water appropriation requirements. The most

---

[39] California Department of Water Resources, *Drought Contingency Planning Guidelines for 1989* (preliminary draft, October 1988), pp. 3–24 and 3–25.

[40] 43 U.S.C. §372.

hotly contested conditions prohibited full impoundment until the bureau showed firm commitments, or at least a specific plan, for the use of the water. Other conditions included diversion restrictions to protect streamflows for fish and wildlife, reservations of water to ensure adequate supplies for residents of the Stanislaus River Basin (where the project was to be constructed), and continuing jurisdiction by the board over the dam's operation.

The bureau sued the state in federal court, claiming that the United States may impound whatever unappropriated water is necessary for a reclamation project without complying with state law. The federal district court and the Ninth Circuit Court of Appeals agreed with the federal government's position, but the Supreme Court reversed.[41] In light of Section 8's "clear language," the court ruled that a state may impose any condition on "control, appropriation, use or distribution of water" in a reclamation project, so long as the condition is not inconsistent with clear congressional directives respecting the project.

This holding was heralded by some as a victory for the states in their authority over water resources. "The *California* decision," proclaimed the deputy attorney general who represented the state in the suit, "has resolved the major controversy that permeated the federal reclamation program during much of its history."[42] Others were not so sure, and the consensus today (if one may be inferred) is that states possess only limited primacy.

When the case came back down to the Ninth Circuit, that court upheld the board's conditions and provided the following interpretation of the Supreme Court's ruling:

[A] state limitation or condition on the federal management or control of a federally financed water project is valid unless it clashes with express or clearly implied congressional intent or

---

[41] *California v. United States*, 403 F. Supp. 874 (E.D. Cal. 1975), *aff'd*, 558 F.2d 1347 (9th Cir. 1977), *rev'd*, 438 U.S. 645 (1978).

[42] R. Walston, "Federal-State Regulations in California: From Conflict to Pragmatism," *Pacific Law Journal*, vol. 19 (1988): 1299, 1320.

works at cross purposes with an important federal interest served by the congressional scheme.[43]

Still, no one is quite sure what constitutes a "clear" statement of congressional intent sufficient to override state law. Many of the unanswered questions concern transfers of reclamation project water. Must Congress speak directly to specific issues such as water transfers and instream flows in order to overcome the states' primacy? What if Congress enunciates a federal policy clearly favoring transfers of reclamation water to non-agricultural uses? Will this federal policy override state laws or policies that might block such transfers? What if there is no clear congressional directive—if federal policy amounts to passive acquiescence to transfers? Can states then take the initiative and encourage transfers outside of reclamation areas? Many of the reclamation projects were authorized in the early part of this century, when Congress could not have envisioned the desirability—or complexity—of water transfers from agriculture to other uses. Is congressional silence therefore abstention?

The Department of the Interior's most recent policy statement (reprinted in Appendix B) does not answer any of these questions, but it does demonstrate that the federal government is not planning to be the initiator of innovative water transfers. Instead, the Bureau of Reclamation plans simply to "get out of the way" and let the transfers happen. In the next section we explain why this policy may not be enough.

Selling or Leasing Reclamation Water

As things stand, a farmer interested in transferring reclamation water to others cannot be certain that the proposed transaction is legal. Reclamation law (a deceptive phrase, indicating a unified body of law where there is none) neither expressly authorizes nor actually prohibits voluntary transfers by a reclamation contractor. In practice, isolated transfers are occurring with the

---

[43] *United States v. State of California, State Water Resources Control Board*, 694 F.2d 1171, 1177 (9th Cir. 1982).

Bureau of Reclamation's implicit approval, and some Interior Department officials have recently and publicly stated that they support the concept of transfers. But without specific authorization by Congress, and without a more definitive statement by the bureau on how transfers will be administered (supported by state law revisions to promote transfers), a significant reallocation of federally supplied water seems unlikely.

And yet, even if federal and congressional policy remain inchoate, in recent years a number of commentators have concluded that reclamation water transfers *fundamentally are legal.* One wrote that the apparent obstacles "derive from administrative practice, rather than specific legal mandates."[44] Another pointed out that a policy impeding project right transfers would undermine the original purpose of the 1902 Reclamation Act— to build the economy of the western states by complementing native water sources.[45] A third argued that there is an implicit bureau policy allowing transfers: "Limited transfers to municipal, industrial and other uses from irrigation are permissible under conditions that offer protection for irrigation and which do not incrementally threaten project cost repayment."[46] All agreed, however, that the law must be clarified before such transfers will occur on any significant scale.

Unfortunately, the body of law that has been building around the Reclamation Act for nearly ninety years does little to clarify the issue for evaluating transfers. As one scholar recently summarized:

Since enactment of the Reclamation Act of 1902, legislation affecting the program has been piled on top of the initial statute without codification or clear direction by Congress as to whether a new statute amends an old one. It is difficult now to ascertain the degree to which the 1902 Act still represents basic

---

[44] R. Wahl, *Promoting Increased Efficiency of Federal Water Use Through Voluntary Water Transfers*, National Center for Food and Agriculture Policy, Discussion Paper No. FAP87–02 (1987), p. 25.

[45] R. Roos-Collins, "Voluntary Conveyance of the Right to Receive a Water Supply from the United States Bureau of Reclamation," *Ecology Law Quarterly*, vol. 13 (1987):773, 781–782.

[46] B. Driver, "The Effect of Reclamation Law on Voluntary Water Transfers," *Rocky Mountain Mineral Law Institute*, vol. 33 (1987):26–1, 26–14.

Reclamation policy. Appropriation enactments, which generally do not contain substantive law, on occasion have been argued to do so in the Reclamation law areas. Added to this confusing stack of inconsistent statutes are Solicitors' opinions purporting to interpret one or another aspect of the law, law that may have changed to the point where some of these opinions are no longer correct. Finally, there often are no Bureau regulations which explain terms of law that have taken on more importance in an age where there is greater pressure for transfers of Bureau water.[47]

More specific legal questions have been raised in regard to particular sections of the 1902 act and its successors. First, Section 8 of the original legislation contains an appurtenancy requirement,[48] which may be interpreted as prohibiting severance of reclamation water from a particular tract of land. This interpretation is probably not the correct one—similar provisions in western states' water codes have not been so construed—but the mere existence of the provision may discourage transfers. Some have argued that subsequent legislation (for example, congressional support for using reclamation water for nonirrigation purposes) has repealed this provision by implication. Repeal by implication is disfavored in the law, however, so an explicit congressional statement on this issue would facilitate reclamation water transfers.

A second statutory provision that has raised legal questions is that "beneficial use shall be the basis, the measure, and the limit of the [reclamation water] right."[49] Once again it is instructive to look to western states' water codes to interpret this language. Each code contains such a provision, and many have defined beneficial use by statute. The beneficial use restriction comes into play when a water rights holder wishes to transfer water to another; only the quantity of water that was previously beneficially used may be transferred, regardless of the size of the "paper right." If beneficial use is strictly defined (and if there is no supplementary language regarding conservation), a farmer

---

[47] Driver, "Effect of Reclamation Law," p. 26–12.

[48] "The right to the use of water acquired under the provisions of this Act shall be appurtenant to the lands irrigated"; 43 U.S.C. §372.

[49] Reclamation Act of 1902, codified at 43 U.S.C. §372.

who installs conservation devices may discover that the saved water is not transferable because it was not legally part of the original water right—since the previously wasted water never was beneficially used, it was not available for salvage. While state courts' interpretations have controlled in this area of the law, there has been some question recently as to whether there is a separate (and presumably stricter) *federal* standard for beneficial use. The possibility of a federal standard may discourage transfers of reclamation water, which are subject to federal law.

A third statutory provision which may present an obstacle to transfers of reclamation water is Section 203(a) (2) of the Reclamation Reform Act of 1982.[50] This section provides that the provisions of the act (including full-cost pricing for some irrigation water) will apply to any district which "enters into any amendment of its contract with the Secretary subsequent to the date of enactment of this Act which enables the district to receive supplemental or additional benefits." Arguably, a contract amendment allowing a farmer to transfer reclamation water to nonagricultural use would fall within the scope of this provision. If so, potential transfers would be discouraged because the act's provisions impose significant additional burdens on reclamation water recipients. Again, legislative clarification (allowing this type of amendment without invoking the Reclamation Reform Act, for example) would alleviate some of the current confusion. Alternatively, the secretary of the interior may declare that such contract amendments "do not provide additional or supplemental benefits."[51]

Each reclamation project was given life by an act of Congress, and such authorizing legislation may have also erected barriers to more efficient use. Project area boundary lines and authorized end uses for project water constitute two of the most significant constraints on transferring reclamation water: Most commentators agree that transferring water outside the areas in which Congress authorized project water to be used, or for unauthorized purposes, is very likely to be illegal. As a conse-

---

[50] Reclamation Reform Act of 1982, Pub. L. No. 97–293, §203(a)(2), codified at 43 U.S.C. §390cc.

[51] See 43 C.F.R. §426.5(a)(3)(ii)(G).

quence, cities may have to construct new dams and water transportation facilities when surplus water is available nearby but on the other side of a project boundary. Legislation could remove this significant legal barrier to water transfers, but any new laws must carefully address the concerns of other irrigators in the district. These water users, for example, must be assured that the new water recipients will continue to meet contract repayment or operation and maintenance obligations. The Department of the Interior's recent policy statement on transfers addresses this problem as follows:

> For the purpose of this statement of principles, all proposed transactions must be between willing parties to the transaction and must be in accordance with applicable State and Federal law. Presentation of a proposal by one party, seeking Federal support or action against other parties, will not be considered in the absence of substantial support for the proposal among affected non-Federal parties. . . .
>
> [The Department of the Interior] will participate in or approve transactions when there are no adverse third-party consequences, or when such third-party consequences will be heard and adjudicated in appropriate State forums, or when such consequences will be mitigated to the satisfaction of the affected parties.[52]

It remains to be seen how such accommodating principles will be implemented in practice.

Meanwhile, each reclamation irrigator holds a contract with the federal government, usually through a delivery entity. Contract provisions are extremely important limitations on reclamation water transfers. In the first place, there are as many different types of contracts as there are contracts (over 4,000); one bureau official likened them to snowflakes, as no two are alike. Most, however, have a provision requiring that the secretary of the interior approve every transfer (of the contract itself or any interest therein) from one contracting party to another person. This provision probably is intended to ensure that

---

[52] U.S. Department of the Interior, *Principles Governing Voluntary Water Transactions* (see Appendix B).

substituted parties will satisfy the repayment obligations of the project. The language is worded so vaguely, however, that the secretary appears to have a vast—though currently unexercised—veto power over water transfers. Potential reclamation water purchasers or lessors may be deterred by the specter of arbitrary federal rejection. It would be ill-advised to remove this federal review authority altogether, as transfers do involve potentially significant impacts on other project recipients, but the bureau has recognized (we think properly) that state officials are better suited to evaluating the impact of water transfers.

Broad policy questions remain unanswered, as well. For example, some people object to a farmer making a profit from the sale of cheap federal water—it looks too much like profiteering at the public expense. (In Colorado, farmers have sold permanent rights to subsidized, federally supplied water for upwards of $2,500 per acre-foot.) One scholar in particular has argued that reclamation projects are intended to benefit the farming community within the project boundaries and that allowing one farmer to retain a profit is contrary to this intent: "The money for which a Reclamation project water right is sold or leased . . . does not belong to the seller, but should be recovered by the irrigation or conservancy district—the repayment obligor—to be held in trust and used for the benefit of the present project community."[53] The majority of commentators today, however, conclude that some profits must be allowed to farmers who conserve and sell their project water, as otherwise there would be no financial incentive to do so. With the exception of a small percentage of reclamation contracts, there does not appear to be any explicit legislative prohibition on such profit.[54] (In Part III we suggest means of both allowing and limiting profits on sales of federally supplied water.)

---

[53] J. Sax, "Selling Reclamation Water Rights: A Case Study in Federal Subsidy Policy," *Michigan Law Review*, vol. 64 (1965):13.

[54] For detailed discussions of this policy question see Driver, "Effect of Reclamation Law," pp. 26–28 to 28–40 (concluding that profits should be allowed subject to limitations deriving from equitable repayment obligations), and Wahl, *Promoting Increased Efficiency*, pp. 36–42 (concluding that recovering "windfalls" is difficult in any market and that transfers from agriculture to municipal use will remove some aspects of federal subsidy).

In summary, although some have argued that transfers of reclamation water fundamentally are legal, such transfers appear to be stymied at least by the threat of legal obstacles. To remedy this problem, we recommend changes in federal law and policy at the end of this book.

Indian Water Transfers

In addition to the water controlled by the Bureau of Reclamation, the federal government indirectly controls a great deal of water to which Indian tribes hold legal title. The marketability of Indian water rights is now being vigorously debated—in Congress, among western water users, and on the Indian reservations. Indian tribes possess legal rights to vast amounts of water in the West (over a million acre-feet in the Colorado River Basin alone) and will surely play a major role in emerging water markets. Their entitlements, however, often are no more than "paper rights" of undefined quantity—a situation which creates considerable confusion when tribes wish to sell or lease their water to others. In this section we describe the nature of Indian water rights, outline their gradual evolution into real or palpable rights, and suggest some changes in federal law that could facilitate transfers of Indian water.

Unlike appropriative water rights created under state law, the basis for Indian water rights lies in *federal* law. Tribes need not comply with state law requirements such as diversion and beneficial use to perfect their rights, and their priority dates are usually based on the time that a reservation was created or even before—not the time that water was first put to use. Thus non-Indian appropriators who established their rights subsequent to the creation of a reservation must be prepared for delayed exercise of Indian water rights. At first glance, this policy—which amounts to "grandfathering" the Indians' rights—appears to be a radical departure from the general rule that appropriators may rely on the stream conditions that existed when they began their water diversions—and it is. The discrepancy can be understood only within the historical context of Indian water rights.

The Winters *Doctrine*

In 1888, the Fort Belknap Indian Reservation was created in Montana, with the Milk River forming its northern boundary. The Indians relegated to this reservation had previously roamed over a much larger tract of land, the Great Blackfoot Indian Reservation. As described by the Supreme Court in 1908, the federal government, in moving the tribe to the Fort Belknap lands, intended to change their "nomadic and uncivilized" habits, encouraging them "to become a pastoral and civilized people." In other words, the sometimes fierce native hunters and gatherers of the plains were to be transformed into placid Jeffersonian farmers. Of more practical importance, however, moving the Indians to a much smaller tract of land would free up more of the public domain for homesteaders. Indeed, non-Indian farmers quickly moved onto the relinquished lands and began diverting water from the Milk River for irrigation, establishing appropriative water rights under Montana state law. When the tribe finally asserted *its* rights to divert irrigation water, the non-Indian appropriators claimed priority based on the fact that they had put the water to use first.

The district court, the Ninth Circuit Court of Appeals, and ultimately the United States Supreme Court all rejected the non-Indians' claims of priority. In a case whose important precedential effect was only appreciated half a century later, the Supreme Court concluded that the tribe's water rights were established under federal law when the United States government signed the treaty establishing the Fort Belknap Reservation.[55] As the purpose of the reservation was to encourage agriculture, and as the lands involved could produce virtually nothing without irrigation, the court concluded that, by implication, the treaty reserved for the Indians the rights to this essential irrigation water. The *Winters* case established that Indian tribes hold "reserved rights" to water to fulfill the purposes

---

[55] *Winters v. United States*, 207 U.S. 564 (1908).

of their reservations; priority dates are determined by when reservations were created.[56]

Few realized the significance of this decision in 1908, and Indians and their implied water rights were almost completely ignored as the Bureau of Reclamation planned and constructed water projects throughout the West. The National Water Commission summarized this period as follows:

> In retrospect, it can be seen that [the federal policy of encouraging settlement and family-sized farms on arid western lands] was pursued with little or no regard for Indian water rights and the *Winters* doctrine. With the encouragement, or at least the cooperation, of the Secretary of the Interior—the very office entrusted with protection of all Indian rights—many large irrigation projects were constructed on streams that flowed through or bordered Indian Reservations, sometimes above and more often below the Reservations. With few exceptions the projects were planned and built without any attempt to define, let alone protect, prior rights that Indian tribes might have had in the waters used for the projects. . . . In the history of the United States Government's treatment of Indian tribes, its failure to protect Indian water rights for use on the Reservations it set aside for them is one of the sorrier chapters.[57]

Eventually, the *Winters* doctrine was reaffirmed and elaborated in a dispute over the flows of the Colorado River. In *Arizona v. California,*[58] the Supreme Court accepted the findings of a special master assigned to arbitrate the issue, who ruled that creation of an Indian reservation implies that the United States reserved sufficient quantities of water to fulfill the purposes for which the reservation was created. Accordingly, on reservations created for agricultural purposes, the quantity of a tribe's reserved water right is calculated by the extent of *practicably irrigable acreage* within the reservation, not the historical water

---

[56] Some scholars have argued that a tribe's priority date may even go back to "time immemorial," a position upheld by the Ninth Circuit Court of Appeals in *United States v. Adair,* 723 F.2d 1394 (9th Cir. 1983), *cert. denied,* 467 U.S. 1252 (1984).

[57] U.S. National Water Commission, *Water Policies for the Future* (1973), pp. 474–475.

[58] 373 U.S. 546 (1963).

use or even the "reasonably foreseeable needs" of the current tribal population.[59]

The National Water Commission, in the passage quoted above, alluded to a potential conflict of interest arising from the secretary of the interior's dual roles: trustee for the Indians and overseer of the Bureau of Reclamation. Many of the bureau's projects have encouraged non-Indians to appropriate and become dependent on waters belonging to tribes under existing but unexercised reserved rights. Obviously this position appears to contravene the secretary's obligation to exercise the highest standards of care in his fiduciary relationship with the Indians. It is intriguing—and, for non-Indian water users, undoubtedly terrifying—to speculate about obligations the courts may infer from the federal government's role as Indian trustee. A 1972 case, for example, held that the secretary, in his fiduciary role, was "obliged to assert his statutory and contractual authority to the fullest extent possible" to preserve water for the Pyramid Lake Paiute Tribe.[60] Applying this standard, the court ruled that the secretary acted improperly *even by seeking an accommodation* between the tribe and non-Indian irrigators in the Truckee-Carson Irrigation District.[61]

The reserved rights doctrine (and quantification based on the purposes for which reservations were established) is consistent with the federal government's Indian policies and fiduciary obligations, but the thought of tribes exercising these potentially enormous water rights strikes mortal fear into the hearts of non-Indian appropriators. Accordingly, they have erected numerous barriers—legal and political—to impede tribes' efforts to convert paper rights to "wet water." These barriers, in turn, often prevent the tribes from participating in water markets and thereby reaping economic benefits from their water. "The ulti-

---

[59] As we go to press, the Supreme Court is considering the practicably irrigable acreage standard in *Wyoming v. United States*.

[60] *Pyramid Lake Paiute Tribe v. Morton*, 354 F. Supp. 252 (D.D.C. 1972).

[61] The Supreme Court subsequently softened this fiduciary duty standard in *Nevada v. United States*, 463 U.S. 110 (1983), in which it concluded that the federal government does not compromise its duty to the Indians simply by advocating the interests of reclamation irrigators.

mate water problem facing most Indian tribes," wrote one observer, "is not whether they have water rights, but whether
water will be available when they are ready to use it."[62]

Obstacles to Indian Water Marketing

Many tribes see water marketing as an important source of
economic benefits—a powerful tool in their efforts to achieve
self-sufficiency. In some instances tribes have not put reserved
water rights to use because they lack capital needed to convert
reservation lands into productive acreage. If water could be
transferred to non-Indian farmers (who often own higher-
quality agricultural lands) or to cities, it would be put to more
efficient use and the tribes could enjoy a greater return on their
resources. Indian water markets are certain to be hampered by a
number of legal and political obstacles, however.

First, the federal government's trust obligations require congressional approval before a tribe may transfer its interests in
real property.[63] While there is some authority for tribes to transfer water to non-Indians for *on-reservation* uses if they obtain
approval by the secretary of the interior, it is likely that all other
transfers require congressional approval. So far, Congress has
cautiously approved water marketing proposals in only a few
instances. In 1982, for example, it authorized the Tohono
O'odham Nation in Arizona (formerly the Papago Tribe) to sell,
exchange, or temporarily lease its water outside the reservation
boundaries.[64] The city of Tucson is negotiating with the Tohono
O'odham to purchase 8,000 acre-feet per year on a 99-year lease
basis.[65] Similarly, in 1988 Congress authorized off-reservation
water leasing in the Salt River Pima–Maricopa Indian Community Water Rights Settlement Act. This bill will enable the Indians to lease their 13,300 acre-feet per year entitlement of

---

[62] D. Getches, "Management and Marketing of Indian Water: From Conflict to
Pragmatism," *University of Colorado Law Review*, vol. 58 (1988):515.

[63] 25 U.S.C. §177.

[64] P.L. 97–293, §306(c)(2), 96 Stat. 1261 (1982).

[65] S. Shupe, "Off Reservation Leasing of Indian Water," in *National Resources
Development in Indian Country* (Ninth Annual Summer Program, Natural Resources
Law Center, University of Colorado, June 8–10, 1988).

Central Arizona Project water to cities in the Phoenix area; the cities have agreed to pay $16 million for a 99-year lease.[66]

During the 1988 congressional debate over Indian water marketing proposals, some western congressmen urged that reserved rights be permanently converted to state appropriative water rights upon transfer (even a lease) for off-reservation uses. Others responded that such a provision would be inconsistent with the laws and policies underlying reserved rights, as it would subject tribal water to forfeiture rules and other restrictions in state water codes. Such legislative wrangling explains why tribal marketing laws have been slow in coming.

Another obstacle to tribal water marketing is the rule that the federal government may not violate its fiduciary duties by allowing uses of tribal property that are inconsistent with the purposes for which reservations are established. Some have claimed that transferring water away from the lands for which it was reserved will contradict the very purpose for which these water rights were created—to encourage agriculture and other "civilized" behavior. But most reservations were created with the general goal of encouraging cultural and economic self-sufficiency; surely these purposes are not compromised by allowing a tribe to enjoy increased benefits by transferring water to others, regardless of where it will be used.[67]

Some have argued further that alienation of water rights would deprive future Indian generations of their option to use reservation lands. This plea for preservation of community values echoes the fears voiced by neighbors of farmers who want to market water to distant cities; in both instances these concerns seem valid and must be taken into account. In some cases, tribal traditions and values tend to discourage agriculture—at least large-scale agriculture—so future generations may not miss the irrigation water. But what about the tribe's future municipal or industrial water needs? Can we assume that eco-

---

[66] "Indian Tribes and Water Marketing," *Water Market Update* (January 1989), p. 11.

[67] For an eloquent argument in support of this position see Getches, "Management and Marketing of Indian Water," pp. 542–543, which points out that free market participation and utilization of tribal resources as capital assets unarguably qualify as the types of "civilized" activities that the federal government intended to encourage when it established reservations.

nomic gains enjoyed from today's transfer will be invested to ensure permanent tribal benefits? Of course the answer is no. Probably the best way to guarantee options for future generations is for tribal councils to approve only temporary transfers of tribal water.

Another objection, which underlies most of the other complaints, is a sense of discrimination felt by non-Indian appropriators who cultivated crops, built water transportation facilities, or otherwise invested personal resources based on water that tribes legally own but have never used. Haven't the Indians forfeited this water, they wonder? What about the discrepancies between state and federal water laws? Why can't they rely on the stream conditions that existed when they began their diversions? The law of reserved rights is well established and has been consistently upheld, but this does not alleviate the sense of basic unfairness felt by many appropriators. In fact some non-Indian appropriators, fearing that they will have to begin paying for water once Indians exercise presently inchoate rights, have invented creative arguments to avoid their own transformation from appropriators to customers.[68]

Despite these obstacles, which in the aggregate appear formidable indeed, we believe that off-reservation marketing of Indian water is inevitable. Courts have repeatedly affirmed the legality of tribal water rights, and in many cases tribes would benefit more by receiving the proceeds from leasing their water than by using the water for on-reservation purposes. When tribal councils evaluate the costs and benefits of water marketing and determine that it is in the best interest of their people to go forward with a leasing program, the federal government should not stand in the way. Just as we urge the Department of the Interior to stand clear when states propose innovative transfer programs, we encourage Congress to adopt a similar attitude

---

[68] This may be the primary motivation behind the Metropolitan Water District's reluctance to purchase water from the Colorado River tribes. Until now the MWD has used this water free of charge under its appropriative rights, which are junior to the Indians' reserved rights. The MWD has persistently argued that it could not legally purchase water from the tribes, as this would contradict the laws governing allocation of the Colorado River. A recent article concluded, however, that "there is nothing in the law to prohibit transactions with Indian tribes." See Getches, "Management and Marketing of Indian Water," p. 545.

when evaluating off-reservation tribal water transfers. In sum, Indian water marketing presents a great potential water source, but the concept is far from being universally accepted.

Water Marketing: A Status Report

In the summer of 1989, as this book goes to press, water marketing can best be described as an idea whose time has almost come. In some western states—Colorado, notably—there has been a hot market in water rights for years. (It was actually hotter in the early 1980s than today, due to helter-skelter growth and speculation in water rights fostered by the state's short-lived energy boom.) In other states, such as California, the development of a water market has lagged far behind. On the whole, though, the notion of selling and buying (or leasing) water rights has gained acceptance—especially today, for as we write this, much of the West remains loosely in the grip of a persistent drought. In the near term, in fact, water transfers are the *only* answer to shortages; by the time any new dams can be built, this drought, at least, will probably be over.

Over the past several years, a number of western states have begun to pass laws, or to amend existing ones, for the purpose of facilitating water transfers for urban, environmental, and—in some cases—agricultural needs. Even in California, where a legacy of tradition and federal water rights ownership has inhibited a potentially vast market in water rights, the Metropolitan Water District of Southern California recently broke important new ground by negotiating a large lease of salvaged water (more than 100,000 acre-feet per year) from the Imperial Irrigation District. And the Interior Department's endorsement—limited though it is—of transfers of federally supplied water represents a historic departure from previous administration policy. (Ironically, former President Jimmy Carter, the bane of the western water development lobby, was unwilling—or simply neglected—to give federal water marketing the blessing it has received from Presidents Reagan and Bush, even though it could turn out to be more effective than "hit lists" in substituting for dams which environmentalists find objectionable.) The following pages present a brief state-by-state overview of water transfer activity in recent years.[69]

Colorado

Colorado has the longest history of water transfers of any western state—although, as we mentioned, the action has slowed there recently even as it has picked up in other states. One reason the trading is so active is that Colorado has a limited supply of surface runoff at its disposal—7.7 million acre-feet versus California's 70 million acre-feet—to meet expanding demands.

Not surprisingly, the largest water market, by far, is along the rapidly urbanizing Front Range between Colorado Springs and Fort Collins. Recent prices for permanent water rights along the Front Range have gone as high as $6,000 per acre-foot, with the highest prices paid around Denver. In Colorado, however, what one buys is not necessarily what one gets. Because the state only permits a transfer of the amount of water consumptively used in the past (not the amount specified in an appropriator's decree), the quantity purchased (the "paper right") may be larger than the quantity one can actually divert and use (the "wet water"), so the buyer assumes some risk.

One major impediment to more marketing and higher prices is the Northern Colorado Water Conservation District's policy prohibiting transfers of water imported through the Colorado–Big Thompson Project to areas outside the district boundaries. The city of Fort Collins lies within the district, but Denver, which is adding many more people than Fort Collins, does not; as a result, NCWCD water rights are currently selling for less than $1,000 per acre-foot, a price that reflects the water's geographic imprisonment. If the district amended its policy, giving Denver access to nearly 200,000 acre-feet of nearby water still being used each year to irrigate crops, the price per share would undoubtedly soar. (Unable to bid for this water, Denver has

---

[69] Most of the information on water marketing that appears in this section is culled from *Water Market Update*, a newsletter published by Shupe and Associates, P.O. Box 2430, Santa Fe, New Mexico 87504.

proposed to augment its supply by building the $800 million-plus Two Forks Dam; development costs could reach $10,000 per acre-foot.)

On Colorado's Western Slope, several years ago, expanding ski areas were paying prices as high as $10,000 per acre-foot for permanent water rights, but this market has recently cooled. Elsewhere in the state, prices are much lower—though that situation could change if energy prices soar, making oil shale and experimental coal development worth the risk. In northwestern Colorado, for example, the highest price we were quoted for water rights was $850 per acre-foot.

Colorado is also ahead of most other western states in its policy of purchasing water rights for the environment. The state's Department of Natural Resources has offered the town of Craig and others a total of $6 million for rights to flows in the Yampa River; the purpose is to ensure that these appropriators will not use their water, so enough water will always run in the stream to protect endangered fish. Even the private sector is participating in the water-for-the-environment market: The Chevron Corporation recently donated substantial water rights, valued at $7 million, to the Nature Conservancy (which, under current interpretations of Colorado law, was required to turn the rights over to the state Water Conservation Board) for instream flows in the Gunnison River.

Utah

Utah's water market is newer than Colorado's and it too has cooled lately. The state has amended several of its water code sections to encourage transfers, providing for an "exchange right" and allowing water to be conveyed outside conservancy districts. Most of the action is around Salt Lake City—another burgeoning desert metropolis, though its growth has been nothing like Denver's. Since 1987, the Central Utah Water Conservancy District has held out a standing offer of $164 per acre-foot for permanent water rights. The Salt Lake County Conservancy District has offered a higher price—around $250. The two entities have purchased more than 100,000 acre-feet of rights so far.

Utah has been the site of several notable negotiated transactions, even though the state has not developed a formal, organized market.[70] One transfer dates back to 1972, when the Utah Power and Light Company entered into a forty-year contract with the Bureau of Reclamation for 6,000 acre-feet per year from the bureau's Emery County Project. Water formerly used for irrigation was converted to industrial use, supplying a coal-fired thermoelectric power plant located 150 miles southeast of Salt Lake City. The deal benefited all of the parties: In return for reducing their allotments of project water, two irrigation companies were relieved of their obligations to repay corresponding project costs. The United States, moreover, received $120,000 per year from the power company (at $20 per acre-foot per year), plus an increased repayment commitment because the project water use was changed from irrigation to industrial. Another coal-fired power plant stimulated a water rights sale in 1980; the Intermountain Power Project paid $1,750 per acre-foot for permanent transfer of 45,000 acre-feet of water rights owned by irrigation companies near Delta, Utah.

Actually, Utah's mutual irrigation companies have allowed market exchanges of water between their shareholders since the days of Mormon pioneers. As many as 90 percent of mutual company shareholders have participated in voluntary purchase or sale of water (or rental) on a seasonal basis. These transactions are facilitated by the fact that water shares are privately held and are not appurtenant to an irrigator's land. (In many cases, however, transfers outside a company's service area are prohibited.) Permanent rights to mutual company water sell for approximately $250 to $336 per acre-foot; the water may be leased for anywhere from $6 to $41 per acre-foot per year.

Arizona

Arizona's landmark 1980 Groundwater Management Act (enacted after considerable pressure from the Carter administration for groundwater law reform) encourages water marketing in a unique way: It requires all developers within a designated

---

[70] The "isolated, negotiated transactions" mentioned here were described in R. Wahl and F. Osterhoudt, "Voluntary Transfers of Water in the West," in U.S. Geological Survey, *National Water Summary 1985*, pp. 113–124.

Active Management Area (AMA) to prove they have an assured 100-year supply of water before they can build new homes. Some developers are putting their faith in the recently completed Central Arizona Project, even though Arizona's share of the overappropriated Colorado River is almost certain to decline steadily, as Upper Basin projects—protected by the Colorado River Compact—are built.[71] But others are purchasing lands with water rights in rural areas and holding them, an activity known as water ranching. (The City of Prescott, for example, recently signed a one-year purchase option on a $15 million water ranch in Big Chino Valley, 50 miles outside the city limits. No one is sure how much water the city will be able to extract from the ranch, but this is one of the largest water ranch purchases to date in Arizona.) Investors, both in-state and out-of-state, are finding the market in Arizona water "futures" more and more attractive as water ranching forges ahead.

Today there is an active market for Type II water rights (groundwater) in both the Phoenix and Tucson area AMAs. Prices have fluctuated from $600 per acre-foot in 1984 to $1,400 in 1986 to around $900 in 1989. One reason for the recent decline is a new state policy requiring more use of treated sewage for highly consumptive urban applications—watering golf courses and so on. There was also quite a bit of speculation going on when prices hit $1,400.

One crucial unresolved issue in Arizona is the dispensation of large unused water rights accruing to several Indian tribes under the *Winters* doctrine. (As we mentioned in the foregoing section on Indian water rights, the focal point of the debate is whether tribal water may be marketed for off-reservation uses.)

New Mexico

In New Mexico, when water rights are sold, the quantity marketed is based on the *consumptive* rather than the diversionary

---

[71] In a severe drought, California gets 4.4 million acre-feet of the Lower Basin's allocation before Arizona receives a drop. This is the "California Guarantee," attached as a rider to the Central Arizona Project's authorizing legislation to win the grudging acquiescence of that state's congressional delegation. It is *another* reason why, in lean times, the project's aqueduct may be half-filled at most.

right. The state engineer's adjustments for consumptive use, in other words, are factored into the amount transferred; thus the buyer assumes less of a risk than in Colorado, since the quantity one buys rights to is very likely to be the quantity one receives. Moreover, since the state engineer uses unvarying formulas to determine consumptive use—instead of making calculations on a case-by-case basis, as the Colorado state engineer does—transaction costs are generally lower. And New Mexico's decision not to adopt Colorado's complex, expensive scheme of third-party injury arbitration (the water courts) has held transaction costs lower still.

Despite such built-in, cost-saving efficiencies, New Mexico's water market has been somewhat slower to develop than Colorado's, mainly because urban growth has been less dramatic. The only sizable city in the state is Albuquerque, an active purchaser of water rights; it has made a standing offer of $1,000 per acre-foot for rights in the Rio Grande watershed. Prices were temporarily higher in the Gila–San Francisco Basin, where industrial users bought up permanent water rights for $3,000 per acre-foot in the 1970s. (The price has recently declined to under $2,000.) Other privately developed water rights in the state are trading for $1,200 to $2,400 per acre-foot.

California

Despite its spectacular population growth (almost 6 million new people since 1980) and the fact that not a single significant new reservoir has been built since then, California has been slow to enter the arena of water transfers. The main limiting factor is the vast amount of federal water (about 12 million acre-feet) tied up in delivery contracts for the Central Valley Project and the Imperial and Coachella Irrigation Districts. Another 2.5 million acre-feet is tied up by State Water Project (SWP) contracts; many of these contracts contain provisions that purport to restrict or prohibit water transfers. (Interestingly, one recent proposal—an offer of rights to 50,000 acre-feet of SWP entitlement water from the Berrenda-Mesa Water District to metropolitan Los Angeles—was rejected by the Kern County

Water Agency, which distributes SWP water to Berrenda-Mesa; KCWA did not want any water leaving its district, under which Berrenda-Mesa is subsumed.)

As far as we can determine, no permanent Central Valley Project (CVP) or Imperial Irrigation District (IID) water rights have been sold to date. However, the Metropolitan Water District (MWD) of Southern California recently negotiated with IID a sale of water conservation technology and management expertise; the water savings are expected to be at least 100,000 acre-feet per year, and MWD has first call on this water for the duration of the agreement. Though this is clearly a market transaction, both MWD and IID steadfastly maintain that it is not a "sale," not "water marketing." The Reagan and Bush administrations both gave their blessings to this concept, which was under intense and sometimes bellicose discussion for nearly four years. A private negotiating team was finally called in to frame the terms and conclude the deal.

Today the most active California water market is in the Los Angeles Basin, where groundwater rights have been completely adjudicated and are administered by MWD in a common pool. Prices for temporary use (sale of water on a year-by-year basis, but not of permanent water rights) have been in the neighborhood of $100 to $150 per acre-foot per year. Elsewhere in the state, one can point to experiments with all kinds of water transfers *except* outright purchases of permanent water rights. Temporary transfers of water between farmers within districts are fairly common in California. The state Department of Water Resources, for its part, recently spent $31.4 million to acquire lands in the Kern River Fan area, where it plans to inject "surplus" flows of Sacramento–San Joaquin Delta water into the underlying aquifer for use in drought years. Eventually the so-called Kern Water Bank is expected to store up to 5 million acre-feet for urban use during droughts. Similarly, the East Bay Municipal Utility District in the Bay Area has offered irrigators using Mokelumne River water (which East Bay MUD shares with them) $50 an acre-foot for water leased in years deemed critically dry by the Department of Water Resources. This offer was formally rejected once, but local irrigation districts are now reconsidering it. (A similar deal was being discussed, in the summer of 1989, by Santa Clara County and the Yuba County Water Agency.) There has even been an offer from Solano County to buy the Bureau of Reclamation's Berryessa Reservoir, which can hold 1.6 million acre-feet of water.

Thus far, all this fertilization has borne little fruit. But with four low-value or surplus crops—rice, pasture, alfalfa, and cotton—consuming more than 14 million acre-feet of water per year (enough for 70 million domestic users), and a projected population of 40 million people in the year 2015, one can safely predict that California's water market will show much more activity in the future.

Nevada

There is a long-standing water rights market in the Reno–Sparks area, where a meager aquifer and one small river—the Truckee—are virtually the only available sources of water to supply a rapidly growing municipal and industrial sector. When there was only one buyer (Sierra Pacific, the local utility), permanent water rights did not sell for much more than $100 per acre-foot. But when both the city and county began actively seeking water rights, prices jumped to around $2,500 per acre-foot. Indeed, Washoe County (where Reno and Sparks are located) entered the water market in a big way in 1988 by signing a $2.05 million option to purchase rights to as much as 10,000 acre-feet of underground water from a ranch in the Honey Lake Basin, about 40 miles north of Reno. Today, as developers have entered the market and driven up prices even farther, the cities of Reno and Sparks have pulled out of the market.

The Stillwater National Wildlife Management Area near Fallon has been plagued by shrinking inflows and contamination caused by upstream irrigation farming along the Truckee and Carson rivers. Because of the refuge's great importance to Pacific Flyway waterfowl, Congress recently authorized $1.2 million for water rights to augment streamflows into Stillwater—possibly an important precedent. A bill recently drafted by Nevada Senator Harry Reid would authorize $16 million for the purchase of additional rights.

Idaho

Idaho's answer to water marketing has, in the main, been water banking—leasing rights to use water for a limited period. Introduced during the drought of the 1970s, Idaho water banking was intended primarily to redistribute federal project water from areas of surplus to areas of deficit—or from areas of low demand to those where demand is higher.

The upper Snake River Basin Water Bank distributes water from four reclamation projects. The district water master, aided by a computerized, hydrological record-keeping system, is compensated by a $0.50 per acre-foot brokerage fee. Water is available for nonirrigation purposes, but irrigators have priority. Idaho Power Company rents more than 95 percent of the available water (using it for hydropower production), buying it at a dirt-cheap price of approximately $2.50 per acre-foot. Upper Snake River Basin officials refuse to allow water users to receive any profit from their subsidized federal water.[72]

Other Western States

Pacific Northwest states have been considerably slower to develop water markets, owing primarily to the abundance of unappropriated water available in their streams. Oregon's new water conservation law may stimulate water markets, however, since it authorizes transfers of salvaged water. Washington's legislature recently charged two committees with assessing the state's future water needs. One of the resulting recommendations was to follow Oregon's lead and allow marketing of salvaged water; this is a likely subject of new legislation in the next few years, legislation which will probably include provisions for protecting instream flows.

Montana has experienced negligible water marketing activity, but the state is anticipating increased demands in the future for energy production. Accordingly, in 1985 Montana's legislators enacted a law requiring that large diversions of unappropriated water be made through leases from the state. More

---

[72] Wahl and Osterhoudt, "Voluntary Transfers," pp. 118–119.

recently, however, the legislature rejected a bill which would have allowed the state's natural resources agency to lease water to supplement instream flows. Ironically, by refusing to take steps to protect flows in their rivers, Montana lawmakers may soon have far more drastic instream flow protection measures thrust on them: Lawsuits based on the public trust doctrine are pending, and an amendment to the state constitution guaranteeing minimum streamflows is gaining support. On the other hand, Montana is one of the few western states (others include Oregon and California) which allow a water user to retain control of salvaged waters.

Wyoming has not seen much water marketing, either, although a transaction (mentioned earlier) between the Casper-Alcova Irrigation District and the city of Casper in central Wyoming has received considerable attention. Otherwise, the state seems fundamentally opposed to water transfers; one water law scholar has concluded that the Wyoming Supreme Court has "interpreted Wyoming transfer statutes in an unnecessarily rigid manner, exhibiting indifference to water rights transfers."[73]

Trends and Prospects

In summary, then, there seem to be several preconditions which augur well for an active market in water rights. One is simple scarcity. The states with the most flourishing markets (Colorado, Arizona, Nevada, Utah, and New Mexico) are either emphatically dry or share much of the runoff in their rivers with neighbor states—or both. Aridity alone, however, is no guarantee that a brisk trade in water rights will materialize. Wyoming, a decidedly arid state, is a case in point. So, in a sense, is California. California's most populous urban region (the South Coast) and its most productive agricultural area (the San Joaquin Valley) are nearly as arid as Wyoming or Arizona, but the northern third of the state is much wetter—and that is where much of the southland's water comes from and where it always expects to find more.

---

[73] Gould, "Water Rights Transfers," p. 32.

Obviously, rapid population growth has much to do with helping water transfers occur. The Front Range of Colorado, Reno, Albuquerque, Salt Lake City—these are all places experiencing what amounts to a continuous population boom. Rapid growth fosters urgent demand, and demand creates high prices, and water—as the old cliché goes—always flows uphill to power and money. But California, the great exception, has stood this rule on its head, too. Several, if not most, of the dozen fastest-growing designated metropolitan areas in the country are in California, which adds a population equal to Oregon's every five or six years. Yet California's water market is in its infancy compared with other states (although the Metropolitan Water District has pioneered some of the most innovative marketing schemes in the West—insisting all along that it is not engaged in marketing).

Again, an important reason for California's dilatory pace is the *theoretical* possibility of more water development. Compared to Colorado, which has developed virtually its entire surface water supply, California still lets nearly half its runoff "waste" to sea without having been put to some purportedly beneficial use. New dams face daunting opposition in that environmentally avant-garde state—especially in the north, where any sizable new mainstream reservoir would have to be built. But the theoretical availability of millions of acre-feet of water from the northern rivers has undoubtedly retarded an active water market; until very recently, the Department of Water Resources and Metropolitan Water District invested nearly all their time, energy, and political capital in efforts to get new projects built.

Another reason California lags behind other western states in water transfers is the dominant role in water development played by the Bureau of Reclamation and the state itself. Between the Central Valley, Imperial, and Coachella projects, the bureau annually distributes some 12 million acre-feet of water within the state—more than a third of California's developed surface water supply. The State Water Project can deliver 2.5 million acre-feet or slightly more in a normal year. Thus nearly half the state's surface water has, in effect, been locked out of the marketplace (although certain market arrangements, such as the MWD/IID contract, are now emerging). As we noted earlier, reclamation laws, policies, and traditions profoundly discourage water transfers. Much the same applies to the State Water Project; many of the SWP contracts contain provisions that purport to restrict or prohibit water transfers.

On balance, one could probably conclude that no 'western state has evolved an ideal system of permitting and overseeing water transfers, nor is any one model appropriate for every state. In Arizona, for example, there is no institutional mechanism by which rural communities are protected against economic injury from sales of water rights to faraway cities. Colorado at first appears to have such a system—the water courts—but the judges have balked at extending their review beyond effects on other water rights holders. It is perfectly evident that no state has devised a way of dealing with the chaotic urban growth that may occur when desert cities are supplied— some would say oversupplied—with plenty of water. And no state has yet managed to reconcile its laws and procedures governing water management with the enormously heightened public interest in the environment; for the most part, they reflect decades-old attitudes.

If a private corporation were suddenly to discover that water used for its agricultural operations yields fewer returns than, say, if the same water were used to create for-profit waterfowl and fish habitat, it would instantly redirect its finite supply of water to these latter uses. But state water codes often prohibit such flexibility, even where new end uses of water enjoy overwhelming public support. In California—among other western states—opinion polls demonstrate extremely strong public support for more fish and wildlife habitat and greater instream flows. There is more and more evidence that water left in the stream, or used to sustain wetlands acreage, is of greater economic value than when it irrigates certain crops. And, of course, in 1988 and early 1989—before some late rains arrived— California cities were virtually begging water from agricultural users. But even where transfers have occurred, almost none have been made for the sake of the environment, mainly because of historically hostile attitudes and a legal and institutional system that expertly thwarts change.

In the final section of this book, we will make some policy recommendations which, we believe, could stretch the developed water supply of the western states for many more years, sustaining not just projected population growth and a healthy agricultural sector but a rejuvenation of water-dependent ecological systems as well. We explore first the conservation potential in the agricultural sector—the water savings one could reasonably expect if state-of-the-art irrigation technology were used throughout the region. Then we look at ways to make this happen: amendments to laws and policies at all levels, loan programs, price structure revisions, and so on. Finally, we propose a federal water conservation program for the entire West to help undo some of the deplorable environmental damage that federal water projects have caused.

Part III ▮▮▮▮▮▮▮▮▮▮▮

A Modest Proposal: Modernizing Water Management in the West

THE energy crises of the early and late 1970s taught America that there are two proven ways to achieve much greater efficiency in energy use: through higher prices and through mandated energy efficiency standards. According to one of the leading experts on energy conservation, Dr. Arthur Rosenfeld of the University of California, efficiency strategies initiated since the first OPEC embargo in 1973 are now saving the United States the equivalent of $150 billion a year in forgone energy costs. Even though Americans drive billions more miles each year than in 1973, automotive fuel consumption in 1987 was virtually the same—the result, mainly, of federal fuel efficiency standards for passenger cars. And electricity demand was only slightly higher in 1987 than in 1980, despite robust economic growth and a population increase of many millions.[1]

We can think of no good reason why these lessons should not apply to water use in the American West. The conservation potential is not as high as for energy if all things except the *technology* of irrigation remain the same: the irrigated acreage, the crop mix, and, above all, the doctrine of western water law. But if irrigators are given incentives to switch to less water-demanding crops and to phase out marginal land or land growing surplus crops—and can then sell any salvaged water—the potential savings are spectacular. Before we make any recommendations for policy changes at the federal and state levels, therefore, it is worth looking at the potential water savings in western irrigated agriculture.

The Realm of the Possible

We focus on agricultural water efficiency simply because irrigation accounts for 80 to 90 percent of consumptive use in the West. Let no one doubt that we strongly support urban water conservation programs, however. According to some experts,[2] simply metering the city of Denver could obviate the need for the $800 million-plus Two Forks Dam; inclining block rates would result in even greater savings. In semiarid and arid regions, we do not see how unmetered homes or flat water rates (as they exist in Fresno, where homeowners pay a fixed monthly fee whether they use 40 or 40,000 gallons per day) can be justified any longer.

---

[1] M. Reisner, "The Rise and Fall and Rise of Energy Conservation," *The Amicus Journal* (Spring 1987):27–31.

[2] David Getches, personal communication, June 1989.

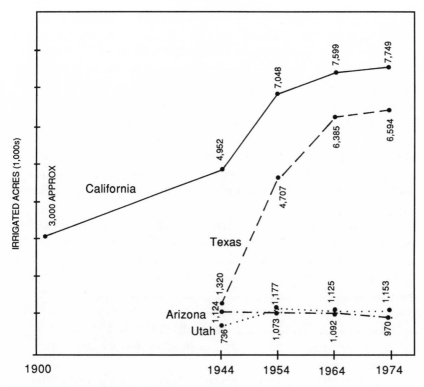

Irrigated acreage in selected western states.

But even if every home in the eleven western states were metered, and even if all consumption beyond, say, 150 gallons per person per day were subject to a hefty surcharge, the water savings would not approach the potential savings in the agricultural sector. One obvious reason is that the agricultural sector uses five to six times more water than the residential and industrial sectors combined. But another reason is that urban users can *afford* to waste water, even relatively expensive water, because frivolous consumption costs them only an extra couple of hundred dollars per year—the price of a ski weekend or a night out on the town. So even very high urban water rates are likely to result in relatively modest savings.

* * *

113

According to the most comprehensive report on irrigation published to date,[3] somewhere between 41 and 45 million acres of land were under irrigation in the United States in 1974, about 90 percent of which was in the seventeen western states. (The figure is undoubtedly higher today, probably more like 60 million acres.) Total irrigation diversions in that year were 177.8 million acre-feet. According to this study, about 41 percent of that amount was consumptively used by crops. Some 46 percent percolated back into usable aquifers or streams, leaving just 13 percent "wasted": consumed by deep-rooted plants (phreatophytes), lost to evaporation, or discharged to the ocean or an unusable aquifer.

As these figures suggest, there is an important difference between reduced *diversions* as a result of efficiency improvements and reduced *consumptive use*. Especially in regions where groundwater and surface water are largely one and the same, and in watersheds where water is beneficially used many times over, one person's water diversion later becomes someone else's supply. So even if a farmer cuts his diversion in half, most of the water he no longer uses is apt to be diverted by someone else downstream.

Moreover, 100 percent irrigation efficiency is, in an economic sense, an impossible goal. Water conservation projects, like water development projects, should generally pass muster through benefit/cost analysis. We believe there are instances where conservation programs with unfavorable benefit/cost ratios should go forward anyway, if essential environmental or cultural values are to be preserved. A flowing river in a desert national park is a priceless asset; even if upriver water conservation is exorbitantly expensive, a real stream flowing through one of the nation's scenic treasures—just as it did in Lewis and Clark's time—is worth the expense. Similarly, we would advocate very expensive taxpayer-financed water conservation efforts in the Carson and Truckee river watersheds for the benefit of the Stillwater Wildlife Management Area, a perilously threatened stopover for millions of birds using the Pacific Flyway. But generally we cannot afford to conserve at any cost.

---

[3] U.S. Department of the Interior, *Irrigation Water Use and Management: An Interagency Task Force Report* (1979).

The most comprehensive report to date that has sought to evaluate both the potential water savings and economic costs of an agricultural salvage effort throughout the West was the study just mentioned, the 1979 *Interagency Task Force Report on Irrigation Water Use and Management.* The report concluded that an expenditure of $14.6 billion on conservation programs would reduce diversions in the seventeen western states by 38.6 million acre-feet and consumptive use by 3.3 million acre-feet. Applying benefit/cost criteria, however, the report recommended a $5 billion program that could free up 2 to 5 million acre-feet. (How a circumscribed conservation effort could potentially salvage *more* water than an all-out effort is not explained.)

These figures compare very favorably with the per-acre-foot costs of water from new dams. (Water development costs at the two largest dams now being seriously proposed in the West— Auburn in California and Two Forks in Colorado—are in the neighborhood of $10,000 per acre-foot in both cases.) Even so, the interagency report suffers from two weaknesses that may bias it against conservation strategies. First, it is based largely on theoretical conservation instead of actual experience; second, the water-saving techniques and technology on which the figures are based are at least twelve years old. Therefore, we think it is instructive to report on the results of what is, right now, the most far-reaching agricultural water conservation program ever launched in the United States.

The High Plains District's Conservation Program

The Texas High Plains, which has become one of the country's richest agricultural regions since the early 1950s, depends almost entirely on the drastically overdrafted Ogallala Aquifer for its irrigation supply. Precipitation is ordinarily 12 to 16 inches per year, and even though much of it comes during the growing season, the area's agricultural output would be very much reduced without irrigation. (Chief crops include cotton, barley, sorghum, and corn.) In the late 1970s, when energy prices almost doubled from one year to the next, the region's farmers realized that they could not afford to pump water indefinitely from a water table that was dropping, in places, as much as 5 feet per year; sooner or later the Ogallala Aquifer would be depleted, at least in an economic sense.

Faced with a drastic phaseout of irrigation farming within twenty or thirty years, and finally despairing of federal rescue— although quite a bit of taxpayer money was spent studying some preposterously expensive water importation schemes—the farmers, under the leadership of the High Plains Underground Water Conservation District, decided to come to their own rescue. The result of ten years of diligent but entirely self-financed conservation efforts has been a region-wide cutback in irrigation water use that ranges between 25 and 40 percent.[4]

That figure, obviously, is much higher than the one mentioned in the interagency report as the maximum theoretically attainable. To some degree, this is because there is virtually no conjunctive surface water and groundwater in the region; what one farmer pumps out of the ground (or "diverts") does not become someone else's adjudicated supply. On the other hand, water in the Ogallala region has for years been substantially more expensive than subsidized federal water; thus one can reasonably assume that irrigation efficiency was already better than on reclamation projects, so the Ogallala farmers had less fat to trim. Without delving into a complex matter of hydrology, we are forced to wonder whether the water-savings potential in western agriculture—through technology and good management alone—is not greater than the authors of the interagency report believe. We turn now to the key features of the High Plains District's water conservation program.

Replacing Unlined Ditches with Pipelines. One of the first and most obvious strategies was the replacement of hundreds, if not thousands, of miles of earth-wall feeder ditches leading from central wells to irrigated fields. These small ditches were as nothing compared to the huge earthen canals supplying water to some Bureau of Reclamation projects, but even so the rate of seepage was very high; losses were often 25 percent for each

---

[4] Most of the information that follows is from personal communications with Wayne Wyatt, the general manager of the High Plains District.

1,000 feet of ditch. Some of the leaked water—referred to as "deep percolation" water—found its way back to the water table, but a substantial amount evaporated, was subject to sub-soil evaporation, or remained suspended, or "perched," between the usable aquifer and the root zones of the crops. The gravity pipelines installed by the region's farmers are mentioned favorably in the interagency report; they are credited with water savings as high as 65 percent. Wayne Wyatt, general manager of the High Plains District, says nearly all the farmers now get their water to their fields in pipes whose efficiency is close to 100 percent.

Improvements in Furrow Irrigation. Although sprinkler irrigation is making rapid inroads across the entire Ogallala region (which stretches from southern South Dakota down to Texas), about half the acreage in the High Plains District is still watered by the furrow method. One of the problems with irrigating a long furrow is that it is difficult to apply just enough water to soak the root zones without flushing through an excess amount that pools, evaporates, and deep-percolates at the end of the furrow rows. Losses as high as 1.7 gallons per minute, per furrow, were measured in the High Plains District—which translates to a loss of hundreds of gallons per minute on a typical field.

The district's farmers largely eliminated such inefficiencies with a two-sided approach. First, many of them have shortened their furrows from half a mile to a quarter of a mile—a distance over which more precise water delivery can be achieved. Most have also installed surge valves on their water pipelines, which shut on and off between rows, sending a measured and relatively small amount of water down the row at a time. With a typical furrow irrigation scheme, a farmer sends the equivalent of a flash flood down his straight, weedless rows; when the initial reach is saturated—or even before if the ground is very dry—the water races through and pools at the tail end of the field (hence the term "tailwater"). The surge valves, combined with shorter furrows, ensure that the least water necessary does the most good. The High Plains District claims irrigation efficiency improvements on the order of 10 to 40 percent from these two strategies alone.

117

Tailwater Pond Improvements. Most water-conscious irrigation farmers recover tailwater and pump it back to the head of the field for reuse. In many cases, however, the tailwater remains standing in fields or unlined ponds for many hours, even days, before being reused. The High Plains District farmers formerly lost as much as 20 percent of the water they pumped to seepage and evaporation from tailwater ponds. To remedy that situation, a majority have now installed small tailwater holding pits and recirculate the water considerably faster than they used to. The efficiency improvement is "substantial," although firm figures have not been calculated.

Soil Moisture Monitoring Devices. Soil moisture monitoring devices—which indicate precisely when a field requires a fresh application of irrigation water—have been around for many years, but their use is still quite rare. The simplest device, known as a gypsum block, is a plaster-of-paris plug fitted with two electrodes; when buried in the root zone of a field and hooked up to an impedance meter, it reveals the relative moisture changes in the water-permeable block and, by implication, the surrounding soil. The cost of gypsum block monitoring (technology and labor) is very low: about $2 per acre. More sophisticated devices called neutron probes—which measure the hydrogen atoms in the soil, indicating the available moisture—are also available. (Indeed, they have been for twenty-five years.) According to a report published by the research organization INFORM, gypsum blocks can yield financial benefits of $50 per acre in the form of reduced water and energy costs and improved yields. At one test strip sponsored by INFORM, a farmer used 30 percent less water on his alfalfa crop—and had he used the technique on his entire acreage, he could have earned $20,000 from higher hay yields alone.[5] Says Wayne Wyatt: "I wouldn't farm without gypsum blocks, and most farmers feel the same way now."

Low-Head Sprinkler Systems. Until the early 1980s, virtually

---

[5] G. Richardson and P. Mueller-Beilschmidt, *Winning with Water: Soil Moisture Monitoring for Efficient Irrigation* (INFORM, 1988).

all the mobile (linear or center-pivot) sprinkler systems used and manufactured in the United States operated under high pressure, sending a fountain spray of water across a field. According to tests performed by the High Plains District and Texas Tech University, up to 60 percent of the water pumped through such sprinklers may be lost to evaporation alone. (Average losses on the hot Texas plains were on the order of 40 percent.) Some years ago, researchers at Texas A&M University took a center-pivot sprinkler, tamped down the hydraulic head, substituted trailing trickle hose for high-pressure nozzles, and found that evaporative losses can be held as low as 2 percent—an efficiency comparable to drip irrigation but usable on almost any crop.

Today, just a few years after the first experiments with low-pressure sprinkler systems, high-pressure sprinklers are virtually gone from the High Plains District. "I haven't seen one in several years," says Wayne Wyatt, "which is remarkable because it took the sprinkler industry several years to come around and begin retrofitting old systems and manufacturing new low-heads. The farmers around here have grabbed them up, because it costs about $10,000 to retrofit one center-pivot and your energy savings pay that back in less than a year." (A new "low-energy precision application unit," capable of irrigating 133 acres, retails for about $35,000.)

A Paradigm of Conservation?

As mentioned earlier, the average water savings achieved by farmers employing all or most of the strategies mentioned above ranges from 25 to 40 percent. Efficient farm managers around Lubbock have reduced irrigation requirements by half—from 36 to 18 inches per year. Vastly improved irrigation efficiency is now so common in the region that the underlying groundwater table, which had been declining by 2 to 5 feet per year all through the 1960s and 1970s, has, against all predictions, lately begun to stabilize. In 1985, there was no change in the aquifer level for the first time in years. In 1986, the water table actually rose by half a foot—the first detectable rise since 1941. In 1987, the aquifer rose by nine-tenths of a foot. In 1988, it declined again, but only by half a foot. Precipitation during those years was normal to above normal, but the rate of natural recharge to the aquifer is so slight that drastically curtailed pumping is almost certainly responsible for much, if not most, of the trend.

The High Plains District's conservation program serves as an example of what is technically achievable in agricultural water conservation. There is nothing particularly unique about the region's soils, and millions of acres of the same crops—cotton, barley, sorghum, corn—are cultivated throughout the West. Admittedly, farmers more dependent on surface water and main canals (rather than thousands of individual wells) would have to employ different water conservation strategies—especially techniques that can deliver water "on demand." In the case of the Imperial Irrigation District in California, the State Water Resources Control Board identified five major (and correctable) water delivery and irrigation methods constituting "unreasonable" use of water and cited a potential water savings in excess of 400,000 acre-feet—which is more in line with the "hypothetical maximum" water savings of 11 to 13 percent for surface water irrigation, but a very substantial savings nonetheless.[6]

What is really unique about the High Plains farmers' case is their near-total reliance on an *unadjudicated* groundwater reservoir. (Or one that, under Texas law, is adjudicated only in the sense that whatever water lies under a farmer's land is his.) Thus few, if any, of the factors inhibiting a major conservation effort in so many western states apply to them. Their water savings are *their* gain (or at least the region's), not some other appropriator's. They receive no hidden federal subsidies that make it cheaper to waste water than to save it. The Ogallala Aquifer is a commons, subject to no interstate compact agreement that encourages the continuation of historic water use patterns.[7]

---

[6] California Water Resources Control Board, *Water Rights Decision 1600*, June 1984.

[7] That states sharing rivers have, by compact, been allocated fixed quantities of water from those rivers would seem to profoundly discourage any water conservation program. (Why make farmers or cities in one state save water so their counterparts in the neighboring state can have more to use or waste?) However, the trend in Supreme Court jurisprudence on compact issues is to reward those states using water more efficiently, at least in the sense of conferring on them a superior equity. For example, in *Colorado v. New Mexico*, 459 U.S. 176 (1982), the court held that "wasteful or inefficient uses will not be protected." See D. Getches, "Water Use Efficiency: The Value of Water in the West," *Public Land Law Review*, vol. 8 (1987):1,25–26.

Does this then mean that no other significant agricultural water conservation program will be launched without a wholesale revision of western water laws, bylaws, and compacts governing interstate water use and allocation? We certainly hope not. A vast amount of irrigated acreage—in the Ogallala region and elsewhere—is affected by the same sort of runaway groundwater overdraft that the High Plains District finally decided to solve or at least ameliorate. "We had some of the worst problems," says Wayne Wyatt, "because the Ogallala feathers out not too far south of here and we don't have the thick saturation they get up in Nebraska. But New Mexico, Oklahoma, Kansas, and Colorado are all looking at the same kind of overdraft we've experienced, maybe a little less severe, and I haven't seen any conservation effort like ours anywhere else." Farmers and cities along the east side of California's San Joaquin Valley are overdrafting groundwater at a rate of 1.7 million acre-feet per year; parts of eastern Oregon and Washington are also mining groundwater at alarming rates.[8] None of these regions is as overwhelmingly dependent on groundwater as the Texas High Plains, but water conservation measures are in their best long-term interest—and in the taxpayers' interest, too, for they may be asked to fund a monumental rescue project when the wells run dry.

Wyatt attributes his region's exemplary success to nothing more than diligence, strong leadership, and state financial support. "Having Texas Tech right here, with its great agriculture program, and it's been very involved, has helped us a lot," he says. "The state loan fund has helped us. But I probably made a hundred and fifty speeches last year selling our agenda to every group that gave me a soapbox. We practiced powerful, friendly persuasion, and it worked. The peer pressure here is great. Any farmer who isn't making a hell of a reasonable effort to save water doesn't have as many friends as he used to."

If the High Plains District's program, and its results, constitute the realm of the *possible*, however, the whole corpus of

---

[8] See the California Department of Water Resources Bulletin 160 Series, published every four years. See also D. Sheridan, *Desertification of the United States* (Council on Environmental Quality, 1981).

western water policy and law still circumscribes the realm of the *practical:* which water conservation effort is workable or economically feasible for a farmer or irrigation district and which is not. And our conclusion—which has been explicit or implicit throughout this book—is that a great many water conservation or water transfer strategies are fenced out of this far more important realm. In the remainder of this final part, therefore, we propose a number of reforms in existing federal and state water law and policy that could significantly, if not radically, change how water is allocated and valued in the arid West. We think of them as a series of guideposts leading the West into the modern water era.

The First Set of Recommendations:
The Federal Level

No matter how serious the Bureau of Reclamation is about changing its mission, it will never succeed without public and congressional support. Bureau of Reclamation projects are, in a very important sense, congressional projects. Every authorization includes specially tailored provisions concerning water contracting and other matters which Congress approves by formal vote. Congress has repeatedly passed amendments to such authorizations—and to the basic corpus of reclamation law itself—that have changed the rules of the game in important ways. In order to encourage efficiency in water consumption or water transfers—and have its actions be strictly legal—the bureau may have to be prodded by Congress, repeatedly, in the form of specific directives and more broadly interpreted powers. We have some suggestions.[9]

---

[9] Another set of recommendations, many of which we happen to concur with, and some of which we have borrowed, is contained in *Water Efficiency: Opportunities for Action,* a report by the Western Governors' Association Water Efficiency Working Group (June 1987). See also B. Driver, *Western Water: Tuning the System* (July 1986), another report published and sponsored by WGA.

Recommendation One

The Department of the Interior should issue a set of rules establishing common terms, procedures, and conditions for voluntary transfers of project water rights. These rules should not, however, impose more restrictive conditions on water right transfers than already exist under state water codes.

We can think of a number of relatively minor rule changes and clarifications that would make transfers more workable:

- Interior guidelines should clarify, first of all, the extent to which one water user may block a transfer proposed by another. As written, the bureau's policy statement on transfers implies that *any* affected party may veto a proposed transfer for any reason. That is a prescription for no water transfers and no increased efficiency.
- The 1988 policy statement says that other recipients of project water must be protected against "diminution in service." This phrase needs better clarification than is provided in the implementing guidelines. Will the bureau authorize transfers so long as project repayment obligations will be met? What about increased operating costs resulting from a smaller number of project irrigators?
- The guidelines should distinguish between a permanent transfer of water *rights* and a temporary transfer of *water* (leases, dry-year options, and the like). Such a distinction could make temporary transfers easier to accomplish. And where potential third-party impacts are unclear, the bureau should permit "trial transfers" which could be canceled if they prove deleterious.

Recommendation Two

Congress should expressly authorize transfers of federal water rights and clarify reclamation law in this regard.

Ideally Congress should revamp the entire program, stating clearly which law or language has been repealed and which executive pronouncements have been integrated into the body of reclamation law. Without such sweeping reform, a few specific changes are nevertheless in order, as listed below. (Once again, the key is to ensure that federal laws do not stand in the way of innovative state water transfer programs.)

- Congress should state definitively that reclamation district lines are not arbitrary boundaries confining project water; transfers outside of reclamation districts should be allowed so long as they are consistent with state transfer policies and do not jeopardize project repayment. Congress should also state clearly that the appurtenancy requirement is not a statutory bar to water transfers.

- Congress should clearly state that end uses of water may always include municipal and industrial supply and environmental enhancement, despite any limiting language in authorizing legislation. (This will prevent objections that such uses are "illegal purposes.") Moreover, the federal "beneficial use" standard should be no more restrictive than the parallel state standards. States should be free to promote conservation and salvage of all irrigation water, including water provided by the Bureau of Reclamation.

- Congress should permit farmers to profit from sales of reclamation water. At the same time, it seems innately unfair that growers who have been receiving subsidized water for a few dollars per acre-foot should be allowed to sell the rights to this water for thousands of dollars an acre-foot. Therefore, some limit should be imposed on a farmer's profit, perhaps based on the difference between his last year's cost and the amount he can get for his water rights. Alternatively, greater profit could be allowed if a certain percentage of the transferred water is donated for local groundwater recharge, environmental enhancement, or some other use that serves the commonweal. (In other words, reclamation farmers might be required to pay an environmental "tax"—in the form of water—in return for permission to enter the water market.) Without permission to make a profit, however, most farmers have no incentive to divest themselves of water rights.

Recommendation Three

Subsidies for federal water should be phased down, surplus crops should be discouraged, and "double-dipping" should be disallowed.

Note that we do not say phased *out*. To many people, a total elimination of federal water subsidies may seem inherently just, but subsidized agricultural water is so much a part of the economic and social fabric of the West that getting rid of it entirely may constitute an unfair burden in itself. We see no reason, however, why the nation's taxpayers, having supplied water to farmers for forty years at a fixed price of a few dollars an acre-foot—and having built up a strong regional economy as a result—should subsidize *another* forty-year contract offering water at an inflation-adjusted price that is even *lower*. (This is exactly what the bureau is preparing to do in the case of the first renegotiated Friant Dam contract, discussed earlier.) How much federal water should "reasonably" cost is a matter beyond our ken. But in California, growers buying water from the State Water Project are paying three to five times more than bureau customers raising the same crops next door— and we see no evidence that State Project farmers are going bankrupt at a rate three to five times faster than reclamation farmers.

• Congress and the administration should investigate ways to end the absurd and wasteful practice—known as "double-dipping"—of offering conventional agricultural price supports to farmers whose crops are already deeply subsidized by reclamation water. (No less objectionable is the spectacle of taxpayer dollars keeping land out of production in the Midwest while more taxpayer dollars subsidize land in the West which raises the same crops.) Congressman Sam Gejdenson (D.— Connecticut) has drafted a bill which would allow farmers to take one subsidy or the other, but not both. It is a reasonable approach: The equity issue and potential water savings are worth the extra paperwork and bureaucracy.

• One approach to conserving water while reducing crop subsidies is to encourage the cultivation of higher-value crops. For some years, crops widely grown on reclamation lands that have been chronically in surplus are, in particular, rice, cotton, and corn. Rice is notorious for its high consumption of water; other crops not subsidized by price support programs—especially alfalfa and irrigated pasture—are also heavy water users and are very common reclamation crops. Most fruits, nuts, and vegetables, on the other hand, are not in surplus and are more thrifty with water. We believe that, since the taxpayers subsidize most of the true cost of federal irrigation water, they should have some say in how the water is used. Several ways to encourage shifts to high-value, water-conserving crops have been suggested:

  · The bureau could reform its rates—as many electric utilities have—to discourage heavy irrigation. For example, the first one or two acre-feet of water (per acre) that it provides should cost much less than the next increment of acre-feet.

  · Farmers with a certain percentage of their acreage planted in permanent crops could receive their full entitlement during droughts, so the burden of shortage would be felt more acutely by those raising nonpermanent crops. (Permanent crops are, almost by definition, high-value crops; their water demand is often, but not always, lower than that of field crops.)

  · The federal government could help finance start-up costs or even install the irrigation technology required when a farmer shifts from field crops to permanent crops or row crops.

  · The Department of the Interior, working with the Department of Agriculture, could mount a much more serious effort to promote commercial cultivation of desert crops in arid regions. If a farmer shifted from, say, alfalfa to jojoba or some other desert-adapted crop, the salvaged water could be sold or leased for municipal and industrial uses, earning the bureau and the farmer more money, and then the desert crop could be irrigated free of charge. Experimental crops, like experimental technology (high-definition TV, for example), may require governmental assistance in order to become established.

126

Recommendation Four

The Department of the Interior should pursue nonstructural solutions to drainage and salinity problems.

Ten years ago, the bureau's answer to the worsening drainage problem on irrigated western lands was to build multi-million or even multi-billion-dollar drainage projects. Since the Kesterson fiasco, its answer has been interminable "studies." But a million acres of farmland in California alone are threatened with extinction, along with hundreds of thousands of acres in other states. Mass waterlogging and desertification of farmlands in the West could present a regional economic crisis that cannot be wished away. In the ancient past, whole civilizations perished because of salinity. A more meaningful policy concerning salinity might include the following elements:

- The most logical way to alleviate the drainage crisis is to reduce the amount of water moving toward impermeable subsoil—in other words, to practice conservation. Yet farmers faced with fairly imminent doom have not done so. Perhaps many still expect the government to rescue them by building drainage systems. On the other hand, reclamation farmers have had little incentive or help in conserving water. All of the conservation-oriented strategies just mentioned would help keep the drainage problem at bay, but it ought to be addressed specifically—particularly in California, where the most valuable threatened farmland is.

- The USDA's Salinity Control Laboratory has conducted experiments on demonstration plots which prove that some crops can thrive on water that has been recycled several times—water far more saline than a normal farmer would use. Cotton, for example, has been grown without yield reduction on water whose salinity content was upwards of 5,900 parts per million.[10] Such demonstration programs need to be expanded to commercial scale. In areas threatened by severe drainage and salinity prob-

---

[10] See J. D. Rhodes and R. D. LeMert, "Use of San Joaquin Valley Saline Drainage Waters for Irrigation of Cotton" (Riverside, Calif.: USDA Salinity Control Laboratory, 1981).

lems, the Department of the Interior should offer a variety of financial incentives to farmers who choose to irrigate under salinity-control guidelines set by the Department of Agriculture. Inclining block rates for agricultural water, mentioned earlier, would also help considerably.

- Thus far the federal government has not found the courage to propose a solution to the salinity problem even more logical than reduced water use—namely, retiring some of the lands that contribute most to the problem. This strategy seems especially attractive in the Colorado River Basin, where farmers in Colorado and Utah export most of the problem downriver to Arizona, California, and Mexico. The Bureau of Reclamation estimates that a 10 part-per-million increase in Colorado River salinity costs Southern California around $6.4 million per year in 1986 dollars; the cost of building and operating the Yuma Desalination Plant could easily top $1.2 billion over thirty years.[11] The bureau, as far as we can determine, has never performed a serious economic analysis comparing such expenses with the cost of buying out and retiring salt-plagued lands—or simply managing them more efficiently. Such a report is long overdue. (One idea is to let the beneficiary states finance the buyout.)

- The bureau should also perform a study calculating the amount of water likely to become available as a result of discontinued irrigation on salt-plagued land. Hundreds of thousands of acres within the Central Valley Project and State Water Project service areas are expected to go out of production within the next half century due to salinity alone (forgetting other factors such as selenium, water and energy costs, and so forth).

Recommendation Five

The administration must address special environmental problems caused by water diversions.

- If the Bush administration is serious about transforming the Bureau of Reclamation into an agency more concerned about the

---

[11] A. Kleinman and F. B. Brown, *Colorado River Salinity: Economic Impacts on Agricultural, Municipal, and Industrial Users* (Denver: U.S. Bureau of Reclamation, 1980); also personal communications, J. van Schilfgaarde, May 17, 1989.

environment, it needs to prepare a priority list of problems caused by decades of water development and diversion and then propose some solutions—with the price and impact attached—to Congress.

- The Department of the Interior should appeal to Congress for funds to conduct a survey of the most serious environmental problems caused by federal water development in the West (and we include projects built by the Corps of Engineers). Then, based on the seriousness of the problem and the potential cost of solutions, it ought to suggest to Congress where immediate action should be taken. We have some recommendations of our own:

  - The Stillwater Wildlife Management Area in Nevada. The historic freshwater inflow into this area has been progressively and drastically reduced by irrigation diversions on the Newlands Project upriver. The refuge is a critically important stopover for hundreds of thousands of migratory waterfowl following the Pacific Flyway. At Stillwater and the nearby Fallon National Wildlife Refuge (now usually dry), 5,200 of the original 79,000 acres of wetlands must support 75 percent of Nevada's ducks, 65 percent of its swans, and over half its geese.[12] The restoration of Stillwater wetlands is of major importance to nearly all the Pacific Flyway states. (One idea is to use a portion of fish and game or other revenues from these states to fund improvements that could, in turn, improve conditions at Stillwater and other vital refuges.)

  - The Sacramento River of California. By far the most important salmon river in the state, the Sacramento has been beset by huge losses of spawning adults and juvenile fish, due mainly to powerful diversion pumps, reduced seasonal flows, inadequate fish screens, and warm-water releases from Shasta Dam. The river is a national treasure—just as its salmon are an important economic resource—and should finally be treated as such.

  - Central Valley wetlands. An astonishing 95 percent of these wetlands, the most important winter waterfowl habitat in North America, have disappeared. The Central Valley Project bears major responsibility for their loss. Today rice farmers along the Sacramento River who wish to flood

---

[12] Freshwater Foundation, *Water Management, Wetlands and Waterfowl: A Blueprint for the Future* (Minneapolis, March 1989).

129

their fields for waterfowl after harvest—rather than pollute the valley's air by burning off the rice stubble—are technically denied water by the bureau on the ground that "creating" waterfowl habitat is not a "legitimate" project purpose (even though postharvest flooding lets rice stubble decompose).[13] Since fish and wildlife are mentioned repeatedly as purposes in amendments to the original Central Valley Project legislation, the bureau's position on this matter seems inconsistent. If legal constraints are indicated, the Department of the Interior should urge Congress specifically to authorize fish and wildlife enhancement as legitimate and coequal purposes of the CVP. Since the project is one of the very few with the capacity to store and release substantially more water than called for by current entitlements, fish and wildlife mitigation is potentially achievable without reducing irrigation withdrawals.

The Second Set of Recommendations: The State Level

Although our primary focus has been on transfers of water from reclamation farmers to cities and the environment, many of the same conservation strategies may be pursued by other individuals holding appropriative water rights. For this reason (and also because state laws profoundly affect movement of federally supplied water) we have some suggestions for western states wishing to encourage water transfers. We recognize that each state has unique water allocation laws and policies, but we encourage states to consider how the following recommendations might be adapted for their particular needs.

Recommendation One

Water transfer laws and policies should be streamlined.

Few state laws explicitly prohibit water transfers or expressly discourage water markets. Many laws and policies, however,

---

[13] Personal communication with Alan Garcia, rice farmer and president of Corning Water District, Orland, California, 1989.

especially those aimed at protecting third parties, effectively inhibit the types of transfers that we believe are desirable. Therefore, states wishing to encourage more efficient water use and transfers must first analyze their existing laws and determine what changes might facilitate beneficial water transfers. (California officials completed such a review a decade ago, producing a useful series of reports on various aspects of the state's water laws and policies.)[14] We have some suggestions:

- Specific changes in state water transfer laws might include refinement of the no-harm rule to establish more specific standards for what constitutes an "injury" to a junior appropriator. Under current laws in some states, a transfer may be delayed (if not blocked altogether) if a junior can show *any* injury, no matter how small. State water codes might be revised to protect juniors against *substantial* injury, allowing transfers to go forward despite minimal impacts on others. Similarly, state transfer laws might be amended to impose a "physical solution," in which an objecting water user is compelled to accept a substitute water source of equal quality or a modification of his diversion—at the expense of the party seeking to effect a water transfer.

- Several states have issued general statements indicating that they favor water transfers and increased water use efficiency. California, for example, took such a step in 1980, announcing that it is "the established policy of this state to facilitate the voluntary transfer of water and water rights where consistent with the public welfare and the place of export and the place of import."[15] While general policy statements alone are unlikely to stimulate water transfers—as California's experience demonstrates—they do provide a useful basis for future legislative changes and may serve as "proof of legislative intent," which could convince a court to authorize a contested transfer.

- All states should reinforce general policy statements with a mandate for ongoing water resources planning—which, as one longtime observer of western water policy has written, "can improve marketability of water by providing reliability, information, and

---

[14] Governor's Commission to Review California Water Rights Law, *Final Report* (December 1978). One of the most helpful preliminary reports is Lee, *The Transfer of Water Rights in California* (December 1977). See also Driver, *Western Water: Tuning the System.*

[15] Cal. Water Code Sect. 109(a).

certainty in private transactions."[16] Without planning, ad hoc water allocation decisions will fail to address the many valid concerns that have been raised in opposition to water markets. Kansas was one of the first states to manage its water under a comprehensive yet flexible water plan; very few other states, however, have taken this important step.[17] We hasten to add that water planning must not be left to the discretion of prodevelopment agencies such as the California Department of Water Resources and the Colorado Water Conservation Board. Perhaps legislatures should empower new planning boards along the lines of the Northwest Power Planning Council in the Columbia River Basin. In any event, citizen participation is absolutely essential; water planning priesthoods have no legitimate role in contemporary life.

Recommendation Two

"Painless" water transfers should be encouraged.

To date, no western state has adopted a policy through which the most painless types of water transfers are carried through first. We think that legislatures should empower agencies charged with overseeing water transfers (such as the California Water Resources Control Board and the New Mexico State Engineer's office) to demand that the least painful means of exchanging water or water rights be negotiated first, perhaps by the following scheme of priority:

- *The first priority* should always be water conservation or salvage. The agreement negotiated between the Metropolitan Water District and Imperial Irrigation District is a model in this regard: Metropolitan has agreed to finance state-of-the-art irrigation efficiency improvements in the Imperial District in exchange for

---

[16] D. Getches, "Water Planning: Untapped Opportunity for the Western States," *Journal of Energy Law and Policy*, vol. 9 (1988):1,8.

[17] A few states, including Montana and Oregon, are developing plans based on the Kansas model. California's water plans have focused primarily on potential water developments, although more recent revisions have included discussions of environmental protection, water use efficiency, and water transfers. These plans are discussed in Getches, "Water Planning."

the right to purchase the salvaged water (which is expected to total more than 100,000 acre-feet per year). In such a way, a substantial amount of water will be freed up for urban use without retiring an acre of farmland.

- If the seller (with or without help from the purchaser) has already made every reasonable effort to irrigate as efficiently as possible—considering his crop of choice, soil conditions, and other relevant circumstances—then *the second priority* should be the negotiation of purchase options during drought years only. In most circumstances, the temporary transfer of water will have fewer adverse effects on local third parties than the permanent sale of water rights and the unrecoverable movement of water outside the district.

- Let us assume that a potential buyer (most likely a city) has made every reasonable effort to negotiate drought-year water leases with farmers whose water could be transferred to the region of demand at reasonable cost. Then *the third priority*—the permanent transfer of water rights—should be permitted. Permanent water rights transfers could also be allowed if farmers or irrigation districts, for whatever reasons, prefer them to drought-year lease options.

- If states find it excessively coercive to enforce such an orderly scheme of transfer—or if it contravenes existing law—then potential buyers and sellers should at least be encouraged by states to work things out this way. States could also adopt nonbinding incentive programs that would help achieve the intended results.

Recommendation Three

Administrative structures and policies should be adapted to achieve a state's water efficiency goals.

Not all reforms require new legislation. State water management agencies possess considerable latitude in their methods of allocating water and adjudicating water rights disputes. Accordingly, individual administrators may play increasingly important roles in facilitating efficient and beneficial transfers. One scholar recently suggested that each state's water agency should view itself as an "involved participant, charged to use its expertise and its information to facilitate efficient decision-making with regard to water rights transfers."[18] In this view, therefore, state administrators are not merely neutral arbitrators; they act more as representatives of the many public interests affected by water transfer decisions.

- Agencies should clarify the conditions that must be satisfied before a proposed water transfer will be approved. For example, an agency may set out the procedures and standards by which a water right will be quantified, so that parties can better estimate the amount of water available for transfer. In New Mexico, the state engineer sets formulas for determining transferable water quantities based on location and crop types; this approach has facilitated transfers by providing parties with an important element of certainty during their negotiations. (We recognize the danger of administrators setting arbitrary formulas.) In other states, such computations are determined on a case-by-case basis, which can be quite expensive.

- Each state could create a water transfer agency or division to match willing buyers and sellers—operating as a water bank— and providing legal and technical assistance for proposed water rights transfers. In 1976, California's Department of Water Resources was directed to perform some of these functions, but widespread transfers did not become a regular feature after the drought of 1976–1977.

Recommendation Four

"Area of origin" protections should be reviewed and modified to meet the anticipated needs of exporting communities.

In Part II we discussed the various options available to states interested in protecting areas of origin when water is transferred to another basin. We concluded that the most equitable

---

[18] G. Gould, "Water Rights Transfers and Third-Party Effects," *Land and Water Law Review*, vol. 23 (1988):1.

methods of protection appear to be compensation schemes rather than transfer prohibitions or reservations of water for speculative future needs.

• States without compensation provisions should consider whether monetary compensation would be feasible and appropriate for the residents living in export basins. States that do have compensation programs should evaluate whether residents in the areas of origin are in fact being adequately compensated for harm caused by water transfers and whether the money is being used to ensure future economic opportunities—not merely to construct unnecessary "compensatory" reservoirs (as has been the case in Colorado) with "river basin" funds. The compensation scheme should be sufficiently flexible to allow for different needs in each area of origin.

• States would benefit by encouraging innovative settlement agreements. Water exporters could, for example, be obligated to reseed retired farmland with native plants, manage them for wildlife—*and* finance weed control at neighboring farms (a major complaint when nearby land is left idle). They could also be required to leave quantities of water in the stream to compensate for lost return flows. By addressing area of origin concerns at the initial stages of a water transfer proposal, parties may be able to agree to such an arrangement without being forced to accept a judicial or administrative decree. (Farmers in the Arkansas River Valley in Colorado reached a mutually satisfying accommodation with the cities of Colorado Springs and Aurora, as we mentioned earlier.) A state may encourage such amicable resolutions by providing for informal administrative proceedings at the initial stages of a water transfer proposal.

Recommendation Five

Instream flow protection measures should be strengthened.

We have described a variety of approaches to instream flow protection, ranging from appropriative instream flow rights to regulatory limits on water rights permits. Since each is adapted to the particular water laws that have developed in each state, it would be pointless to recommend a single approach for protecting instream flows. The few states that still do not recognize instream uses as "beneficial" are the most obvious candidates for statutory or regulatory reform. We have some further suggestions on making instream flow protection more workable:

- States embracing the appropriative rights approach should consider broadening the class of entities who can hold instream flow rights. Perhaps a state with a valuable whitewater rafting trade should allow rafting companies to purchase upstream appropriative rights and convert them to instream flows to maintain their business. A city may wish to purchase instream flow rights upstream from a waste treatment plant, so that pollutants are diluted in the flow. And a conservation group may be willing to "put its money where its mouth is" and purchase the necessary instream flows to maintain a favorite stretch of stream.

- On the other hand, some arguments against privately held instream flow rights strike us as persuasive (see the discussion on page 75), so we caution each state to consider the drawbacks of, and alternatives to, this approach. A state may, for example, prefer public entities to make the choices about which streams to protect. Average citizens who can now participate, at least in theory, in public decision-making may effectively lose this right if decisions are made privately by whoever can afford to buy water rights. And Colorado's scheme, in which individuals may purchase appropriative rights and turn them over to the state for instream flow protection, answers some of these "equity objections." Moreover, there are other means of protecting streamflows—as demonstrated by an agreement concerning timed reservoir releases in New Mexico. (We discuss this arrangement on page 75.) Such innovative private options should be explored in the context of each state's water rights laws.

- Finally—and we discuss this later under Recommendation Seven—instream flow protection can be pursued in conjunction with a program to promote conservation and salvage of water. Oregon's recently enacted program provides an excellent model for other states to emulate.

Recommendation Six

The public trust doctrine must be accommodated by state water transfer laws and policies.

We have described recent developments that signal an increasing concern about the impact of water allocation decisions on many public values (fish, wetlands, aesthetics, rural culture) that historically have been ignored. While some have decried this steady erosion of the traditional protection of vested rights above all else, others have cheered legal changes that reflect today's environmental, social, and economic values. Charles Wilkinson, a leading scholar of natural resources law, concludes: "The recognition of the public trust doctrine in water law is the single strongest statement that historic uses must accommodate modern needs."[19]

- How can states best respond to this trend? Above all, each state should develop specific guidelines to help agencies and courts determine whether proposed transfers are consistent with public values. This task will require a difficult balancing of competing interests and probably ought to be addressed, at least initially, by legislation. Once a state legislature sets out a general scheme for making public interest determinations, however, the state agency that administers water rights would flesh out the details of the program.

Recommendation Seven

Water conservation and salvage should be promoted.

Prior appropriation law must be changed to allow water rights holders to retain control over waters salvaged through improved conveyance and delivery systems or new crop mixes.

---

[19] C. Wilkinson, "Western Water Law in Transition," *University of Colorado Law Review*, vol. 56 (1985):317.

Without the possibility of selling this water for a profit—whether limited or unrestricted—farmers have no economic incentive to curtail wasteful irrigation practices.

- When contemplating these changes, each state must consider the risks inherent in conservation and salvage, including the loss of wetlands and harm to other appropriators who rely on return flows. These dangers may be alleviated by allowing transfer only of "irretrievable losses"—water that never came back to the stream as return flow. As demonstrated by Oregon's new statute and regulations, a state may further protect against downstream impact by requiring that a portion of the conserved water be reserved for enhanced streamflow.

- There is some question, however, as to the effectiveness of this type of legislative change. In California, for example, conservation/salvage provisions have been on the books since the early 1980s, but attorneys we spoke with from the State Water Resources Control Board were not aware of a single transfer whose impetus came from such measures. Oregon's program is simply too new to evaluate at this point.

Recommendation Eight

Unilateral interstate transfer restrictions must be removed.

Recent judicial decisions (particularly *Sporhase*) have established that states may not categorically ban interstate transfers of water. Instead—so this reasoning goes—legal restrictions should be based on valid health and welfare concerns (including water conservation) and must constrain state residents as well as nonresidents. Thus the highest court in the nation has approved the concept of interstate water markets, and states would be ill-advised to ignore the signal. State laws and regulations must reflect this new reality, allowing reasonable transfers and basing all necessary restrictions on rational grounds. States that fail to respond may forfeit their authority to the federal government, which holds a pervasive but currently unexercised prerogative. States may, of course, lawfully limit water exports through compacts with other states.

A Final Recommendation: A Conserved Water Trust for the Environment

We have made a number of suggestions about changes in federal and state laws and administrative procedures which would, we believe, result in far easier water transfers and vastly more efficient water use. But assuming nothing changes for a while, can the Bureau of Reclamation launch a significant water conservation program anyway? We think it can—and we believe it could go far beyond the mere lining of main canals, which is essentially what the agency has proposed to do thus far.

We base our opinion partially on precedent: the Metropolitan Water District/Imperial Irrigation District water salvage program. Assuming this proposed water exchange withstands legal challenges, it means that farmers on reclamation lands can at least *lease* salvaged water by long-term contract to other users outside their district's boundaries. Metropolitan's water right was next in seniority to Imperial's, so Imperial's conserved water was automatically diverted there. But one can seriously question whether the next senior appropriator *must* be the beneficiary of all the water that farmers in a reclamation project manage to conserve.

The statutes authorizing many such projects contain language—either in the enabling legislation or in subsequent amendments—proclaiming fish and wildlife enhancement as legitimate purposes of the project in question, sometimes even coequal with reclamation. Moreover some projects—notably California's Central Valley Project—have already been operated, in isolated instances, for environmental enhancement, even without specific statutory or administrative directives. For example, the bureau has provided substantially more freshwater outflow to the Delta and San Francisco Bay than the State Water Project, even though a strong case can be made that this is primarily a state responsibility. And both the Bureau of Reclamation and the California Department of Water Resources recently agreed to reduce pumped diversions through the Delta during the salmon migration season—even though, during an

139

extended drought, such action could effectively diminish water deliveries to farmers and cities.

From here it is not that big a step to supplying conserved water to rivers, wetlands, and other natural areas inside or outside project boundaries. What we have in mind is something one could call a Conserved Water Trust for the environment—a liquid trust fund, if you will, created by statute or simple administrative rule, that would receive water conserved by participating farmers and lease it to fish, wildlife, and environmental enhancement projects selected by state or federal conservation agencies. Farmers would benefit by seeing their water costs reduced and perhaps from higher crop yields—though some other incentives might well have to be added to make the program work. The Bureau of Reclamation would have its reputation significantly restored—and most would agree that it is currently at a historic nadir. Drainage problems, especially in the San Joaquin Valley of California, might be substantially reduced. (The less irrigation water the farmers apply, the less contaminated water there is to be got rid of.) And Americans, who seem ever more concerned about the progressive deterioration of their environment, would benefit in every way.

A number of electric utilities—notably Southern California Edison—have had remarkable success in reducing demand growth by offering zero-interest loans to customers for energy conservation improvements.[20] We believe the Interior Department should follow their lead and do exactly the same thing. If bureau water is so cheap (and this, by the way, would be a good lesson in how subsidized the water really is) that most farmers would *still* elect not to invest in water-saving technology—even if it is offered to them interest-free—additional incentives could be provided. We have a few in mind:

—All growers participating in the water conservation program might be promised smaller cutbacks during droughts.

—Participating farmers could be promised discounted water rates when their contracts are renegotiated—or they could even be discounted today. (We are aware of no statute that says the In-

---

[20] See M. Reisner, "The Great Big Utility That Could," *The Amicus Journal* (Spring 1985).

terior Department cannot *lower* a farmer's water rate in mid-contract.)

—After a grower spends a certain amount of money on water conservation, the Interior Department itself could finance further improvements up to a given level of expenditure.

—The Interior Department could simply appeal to Congress for funds to finance the entire program at taxpayer expense.

Another idea would be for the interior secretary—in exchange for giving sanction to commercial water transfer proposals such as the MWD/IID deal—to demand that a certain amount of the transferred water be earmarked for environmental purposes.

There are at least a couple of problems with this proposal. One concerns legality. The law on out-of-district transfers of salvaged water is by no means clear, and it may vary considerably from state to state and district to district. When Congress recently authorized the Bureau of Reclamation to concrete-line the All-American Canal, an improvement which is expected to salvage another 100,000 acre-feet of water within the Imperial Irrigation District (in addition to the 100,000 acre-feet that will conservatively be yielded by MWD-sponsored efficiency improvements), it invoked the 1931 Seven-Party Agreement between the major California users of Colorado River water, which it interpreted as requiring that "water that is not applied to beneficial use by a California Contractor is available for use by the California Contractor with the next priority."[21] In such a manner, Metropolitan, which is next in priority behind Imperial, was guaranteed all the salvaged water that lining the canal will yield. This provision was adopted over the vigorous opposition of lawyers for the Environmental Defense Fund (EDF), who argued that any salvaged water should legally be sold to the highest bidder. EDF's argument may have to be tested in the courts, but it seems to hold out the possibility that salvaged water need not go directly to the user with the next senior right—a precedent that would make it potentially available for environmental purposes.

---

[21] San Luis Rey Water Rights Act, Public Law No. 100–675, 102 Stat. 4000, 4005 (November 17, 1988).

Another possible snag is the reclamation law itself, which states that the beneficial use standard is "the basis, the measure, and the limit of the [water] right." At least one case interpreted this phrase as prohibiting the secretary of the interior from spending public funds or supplying water for nonbeneficial uses.[22] Thus enhancing instream flows and fish and wildlife habitat (which are not defined as "beneficial uses" in some states) may be technically illegal. Further, many states still embrace the traditional beneficial use definition, which effectively discourages conservation because salvaged water does not belong to the appropriator. Because the Bureau of Reclamation defers to state allocation laws, this interpretation could create problems in states other than California, Oregon, and Montana, which have amended their laws to allow continued control over conserved water. All these concerns, however, are easily addressed by legislation or administrative policy reform.

Another problem with our proposal is that reduced agricultural water consumption would also stanch the flow of money going into project repayment coffers. Repayment from irrigators, however, usually amounts to a fairly minimal share; power revenues and municipal and industrial water sales keep most of these projects financially afloat. Also, to some degree, this effect might be offset by reduced operation and management costs and a new surplus of power the bureau could sell at premium rates. (As farmers use less water, electricity needed for pumped diversions declines—and remember that power used for pumping irrigation water is sold at subsidized, rather than market, rates.)

Taking the role of devil's advocate still further, one can safely predict that junior diverters or those who rely on return flows will complain that any water conservation program is bound to upset the flow regimes on which they have come to depend. Obviously, though, these objections were somehow satisfied in the MWD/IID deal, which is very much like our Conserved Water Trust idea; the main difference is that water conserved in the Imperial District will be sold to urban Southern California rather than used for environmental enhancement. There is no

---

[22] *Fox v. Ickes*, 137 F. 2d 30 (D.C. Cir. 1943), *cert. denied*, 320 U.S. 792 (1943).

reason, moreover, why the Interior Department (perhaps through the Land and Water Conservation Fund) or Congress cannot compensate farmers who make serious efforts to conserve precious water for wildlife and the environment.

The main point is that the Bureau of Reclamation, the Interior Department, and the Congress, by authorizing and building hundreds of federal water projects, are collectively responsible for a staggering loss of aesthetic beauty and wildlife and fish habitat over the years. To earlier generations of Americans, enjoyment of these wild resources was almost a birthright. Are we simply going to declare this habitat, and the wild creatures that depended on it, forever lost? Or are we going to try to create an opportunity for taxpayer-subsidized western agriculture to make amends for the damage it has caused?

Conclusion

I T is ironic that water development in the American West—which was accomplished only through a sharp break with economic, legal, and cultural tradition—has now become a hidebound tradition in its own right, deeply resistant to change. When pioneers began settling the arid West, they immediately overthrew the traditional doctrine of riparian water law and substituted the radically different appropriative rights doctrine in its place. By creating the Bureau of Reclamation, Congress handed radical new powers to itself and the executive branch and launched a wholly new experiment in agrarian pseudosocialism. We do not suggest that this course was unwarranted or wrong. It was necessary and inevitable, at least to some degree, if our ancestors were serious about booting the Native Americans off their land and transforming a vast portion of the continent that had proved hostile or indifferent to their material aspirations.

On the other hand, that water development in the West has been a remarkable *economic* success, and has served the nation

145

well, certainly does not mean it should be declared off-limits to reform. Western water law promotes stability by being quite intolerant of change; it discourages efficiency in water use and implicitly recognizes irrigated agriculture as sacrosanct. The federal government—through the Bureau of Reclamation, at least in its historic incarnation—does much the same thing. Today, however, as David Getches has written, "society benefits from making fuller, more productive use of water resources, not from rigorous obeisance to an awkward system that defines water rights based on historical practices."[1]

In our view, the Bureau of Reclamation need not be abolished (though the idea deserves careful thought) nor the doctrine of western water law scrapped. In the West, the scarcity of water is such an overwhelming and immutable reality that the bureau, subsidized agriculture, and many tenets of existing law may be with us forever. But after a century of very little substantive change in the way Americans allocate, develop, and even think about water, we believe it is long past time for historic reform. Our approach to western water is now very much at odds with environmental protection, which has become one of society's greatest concerns. It is at odds with the free market economic system, whose fundamental efficacy has been rediscovered by Democrats and Republicans alike. It cuts against the grain of America's oldest public virtue: Yankee thrift and efficiency.

We do not expect or advocate overnight change. But a lot can happen in a few years. American cars now travel nearly twice as far on a gallon of gas as in 1973, and they are safer, better built, and fast enough. Between 1976 and 1981, the Tennessee Valley Authority and Bonneville Power Administration both metamorphosed from agencies utterly obsessed with power generation into two of the world's leading governmental bodies involved with energy efficiency and conservation. The Bureau of Reclamation, on the other hand, is still very much like the Bureau of Reclamation: its "new mission" largely undefined, its new priorities still unclear or greatly hampered by policies and laws it has not moved to change. And the western states, for their

---

[1] D. Getches, "Water Use Efficiency: The Value of Water in the West," *Public Land Law Review*, vol. 8 (1987):1,16.

part, have not responded well (with some notable exceptions) to the sweeping changes of the past two decades: the shriveling importance of the agricultural economy, the explosive growth of water-short cities, the desperate deterioration of water-dependent ecosystems, and the environmental concerns that the vast majority of their own citizens now share.

And yet it is in the case of western water that one of the most interesting lessons of modern times is being learned—that free market economics and environmental preservation are not nearly so incompatible as many have thought. Allowing water in the West to gravitate to its highest economic use could be enormously beneficial to rivers, wetlands, wildlife, and whole ecosystems. But a more rational scheme of priority, allocation, and end use has been subverted by a system almost Soviet-like in its inefficiency, its unyielding laws, its abrogation of power to a distant priesthood of planners and lawyers and engineers whose attitude toward nature, not to say efficiency, seems one of indifference—or, at best, passing interest.

Our book is little more than a map through the great morass that is western water tradition, policy, and law. We have recommended changes—new policies, new priorities, new laws, even new kinds of subsidies—that may or may not work but deserve to be tried. Now it is time for westerners to do something they have rarely done in the case of water management, except where their own proprietary interests are at stake: get involved. Without public support for change, change is almost certain not to occur.

The water users in the West, after all, merely borrow it from the public at large; fundamentally, the water belongs to everyone.

Can America get through the next thirty, forty, or fifty years without building any more major dams in the West? The answer is yes. In theory, on paper, it is quite possible. In practice, in real life, it poses a challenge at least as daunting as the drafting of the laws, the negotiation of the compacts, and the construction of the dams themselves.

Appendix A

The Imperial Irrigation District/ Metropolitan Water District Water Transfer: A Case Study

<blockquote>
"Simple ain't easy."
—*Thelonius Monk*
</blockquote>

For a variety of reasons, some more obvious and some less rational than others, water marketing has not prospered in California as it has in other western states—even though there are a number of reasons why it should. For one thing, a great deal of water has been developed—close to 40 million acre-feet. A lot of it is used to irrigate relatively low-value crops. Nearly a third of the water is heavily subsidized by the federal government, implying some degree of inefficiency. And urban growth (and its demand for more water) has continued relentlessly in recent years. As more than one observer has pointed out, the failure of an active water market to emerge has more to do with political resistance from the agricultural community—and with uncertainty about who has what to

This case study was adapted from a paper prepared by 1989 Hastings law graduates Jeffrey W. Schwarz and Kimberly Martin McMorrow for a seminar taught by Professor Brian Gray, University of California, Hastings College of the Law.

sell—than with insuperable obstacles presented by federal, state, or water district laws and bylaws. The question, then, is this: Given California's historic resistance to the *idea* of water marketing, how can water transfers be pragmatically achieved? The recent agreement between the Metropolitan Water District and the Imperial Irrigation District may well be the model to emulate. Neither a true sale of water rights nor a conventional lease of water, this creative—and probably historic—water salvage arrangement deserves careful scrutiny.

Background

The Metropolitan Water District

The Metropolitan Water District (MWD) of Southern California holds pre-1914 appropriative water rights and provides water to approximately 14.1 million residents of the southern coastal region of California.[1] During the 1986–1987 fiscal year, MWD sold approximately 1.75 million acre-feet. Of the 4.4 million acre-feet per year adjudicated to California by the United States Supreme Court in *Arizona v. California*,[2] the California Seven-Party Agreement gives MWD a fourth priority right to 550,000 acre-feet a year.[3] Subject to superior rights of Palo Verde, Yuma, Imperial, and Coachella, which together hold the first priority right to 3.85 million acre-feet a year, and the amount of water in the Colorado River in a given year, MWD has a fifth priority right to an additional 662,000 acre-feet for a total of 1.2 million acre-feet per year.[4] Because of the wet conditions prevailing in the Colorado River Basin since 1983, however, MWD has diverted closer to 1.3 million. Thus, by 1992, when the Central Arizona Project is scheduled to divert 2.8 million acre-feet a year of Colorado River water, MWD will face a potential systemwide shortfall during dry periods of 560,000 acre-feet a year by the year 2000, increasing to 980,000 acre-feet by 2010.

---

[1] Bulletin 160–87, *California Water: Looking to the Future*, Department of Water Resources (November 1987), p. 6.

[2] 373 U.S. 340 (1964).

[3] State Water Resources Control Board Decision 1600 (June 21, 1984), pp. 11–12; hereafter cited as Decision 1600.

[4] Decision 1600, pp. 11, 53.

The Imperial Irrigation District

Encompassing 1,062,290 acres, of which 460,000 acres are irrigated, the Imperial Irrigation District (IID) diverts 2.9 million acre-feet a year of Colorado River water, the most of any user in California.[5] Imperial not only provides water to agricultural users whose gross sales output exceeded $757 million in 1980, but also functions as an electrical utility for virtually all of Imperial County, as well as a large part of Riverside County. Imperial holds pre-1914 appropriative water rights[6] and a present perfected right to divert the lesser of 2.6 million acre-feet a year or the quantity of water reasonably needed to supply consumptive and related uses on 424,125 acres. To the extent that Palo Verde and Yuma do not fully use their allotment, IID may divert an additional 300,000 acre-feet for a total of 2.9 million acre-feet a year.[7]

Proceedings

On June 17, 1980, John Elmore, an Imperial County farmer, requested that the Department of Water Resources (DWR) investigate alleged misuse of water by IID. Elmore contended that excessive water deliveries to agricultural users resulted in large quantities of tailwater flowing into the highly saline Salton Sea, causing it to overflow its banks and inundate his land. DWR's investigation indicated that 438,000 acre-feet a year could be conserved through a combination of operational and physical improvements to IID's water delivery systems.[8] DWR therefore ordered IID to submit a detailed water conservation plan. Although IID initially agreed to prepare such a plan, it later notified DWR on September 29, 1982, of its refusal to comply with the order, stating

---

[5] Decision 1600, pp. 5, 52.

[6] Imperial acquired its water right during the later nineteenth century by "posting" its diversion at Hanlon's Heading on the Colorado River and then putting the water to beneficial use. This state-perfected right is owned by IID, which acts as the trustee of the water for the individual landowner beneficiaries. When the Boulder Canyon Project Act took effect in 1929, IID was diverting, transporting, and delivering Colorado River water to 424,145 acres through its privately owned water delivery system. Under the Project Act and a 1932 implementing contract, the United States constructed and IID agreed to help pay for a new delivery system. IID's present perfected right was recognized by the United States Supreme Court in *Arizona v. California*, 373 U.S. 340 (1964), and also in *Bryant v. Yellen*, 447 U.S. 350 (1980).

[7] Decision 1600, p. 13.

[8] Decision 1600, p. 3.

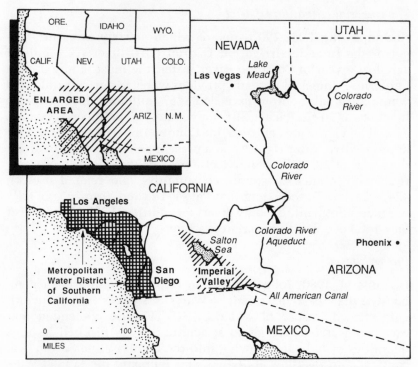

Source: IID Draft EIR: *Proposed Water Conservation Program and Initial Water Transfer,* April 1986, Figure 2-1.

The Metropolitan Water District and Imperial Irrigation District in southern California.

that its use of Colorado River water was reasonable and preparation of the plan unjustified.[9]

At the conclusion of DWR's investigation, Elmore requested a hearing in front of the State Water Resources Control Board. (He later brought suit against IID for damages and injunctive relief and petitioned for a writ of mandamus seeking adjudication of the allegations that IID violated its duty not to waste and misuse water.) The board heard the matter in September and December 1983 and issued Decision 1600 on June 21, 1984.

In Decision 1600 the board found that IID's failure to implement

---

[9] The issue as far as IID was concerned was one of "need." How could there be waste and unreasonable use of water when there was no need for it? During the early 1980s, IID argued that MWD's aqueduct was full and that any water IID could have "conserved" would have wasted to the Gulf of California.

additional water conservation measures was unreasonable and a misuse of water under Article X, Section 2, of the California Constitution, which "requires that water resources of the State be put to beneficial use to the fullest extent of which they are capable." IID was ordered to submit evidence to the board by February 1, 1985, regarding tailwater monitoring, repair of defective tailwater structures, plans for resuming construction of regulatory reservoirs, development of an improved water accounting system, and preparation of a comprehensive water conservation plan specifying a schedule of implementation and method of financing certain water conservation measures.

The board relied on DWR's estimate of IID losses and determined that the quantity of water IID ultimately would be required to conserve would depend on the rate of development of the Central Arizona Project, the water usage of other parties to the Seven-Party Agreement, and the future salinity of the Colorado River.

On September 20, 1984, the board denied IID's request for reconsideration of Decision 1600.[10] IID then challenged the board's authority to adjudicate the reasonableness of its water use under pre-1914 appropriative water rights and its authority to order corrective measures, in an action for declaratory relief. The Court of Appeal reversed the trial court's decision on November 4, 1986, and held that the board was authorized to adjudicate claims of unreasonable use and to order corrective action where misuses of water are found. The California Supreme Court denied IID's petition for review and the case was remanded to Superior Court. On April 13, 1988, the Superior Court held that the evidence amply supported the board's finding in Decision 1600 that the failure of IID to implement additional water conservation measures was unreasonable and constituted a misuse of water under Article X, Section 2, of the California Constitution. The court then remanded the case to the board to establish a new schedule for compliance with Decision 1600.

Meanwhile, IID spent millions of dollars on conservation studies to comply with Decision 1600 and many of the district's agricultural customers installed concrete head ditches and tile systems to eliminate the effects of saline subsurface water. Indeed, IID says it would have voluntarily undertaken more conservation measures but its limited resources prevented its members from doing so. Clearly, the California Supreme Court's denial of IID's petition of review forced IID to pursue water transfer negotiations.

---

[10] *IID v. State Water Resources Control Board*, 186 Cal. App. 3d 1160 (4th Dist. 1986).

Negotiations

When California voters rejected the Peripheral Canal proposition in June 1982, MWD was forced to pursue alternative long-term water supply contracts to compensate for its reduced entitlement to Colorado River water caused by the Central Arizona Project going on line in late 1985. In March 1983, the Environmental Defense Fund (EDF) produced a detailed proposal whereby MWD would finance IID water conservation measures and, in return, be given the right to use the salvaged water.[11] Using the 1981 Department of Water Resources estimate that 437,000 acre-feet a year of Colorado River water could be conserved within the Imperial District, EDF concluded that it was both economically and legally feasible for IID to transfer conserved water to MWD. (Indeed, MWD had discussed the possibility of obtaining water from the Imperial Valley since the early 1970s. Because there was little transfer activity in the state at the time and IID was not interested in a trade, the discussions were not fruitful.)

EDF's 1983 proposal was not met with much enthusiasm from IID agricultural users—who had little incentive to conserve cheap water and who feared that such a proposal would jeopardize their entitlement to Colorado River water.[12] But mounting pressure from John Elmore's lawsuit persuaded IID to explore the idea of a proposed water transfer with MWD and in January 1984 the Imperial District voted to begin negotiations. Thus, on April 12, 1984, slightly more than a year after EDF's proposal was completed, officials from IID and MWD met for the first time to discuss a water trade.

In 1985, Parson's Water Resources Inc. completed a water transfer study which concluded that MWD was the most suitable candidate for a water transfer agreement because it had the necessary facilities and conveyance capacity as well as an existing contract for Colorado River water—which meant it was familiar with water contract administration policies of the Department of Interior. By July 1985, MWD and IID had drafted a memorandum of understanding whereby MWD would pay $10 million annually into IID's Water Conservation Fund; in return, MWD would receive a firm

---

[11] Environmental Defense Fund, *Trading Conservation Investments for Water* (March 1983).

[12] IID does not pay the federal government for its water right. Under the Reclamation Act of 1902 and the Boulder Canyon Project Act, IID and the federal government

annual supply of 100,000 acre-feet of conserved IID water. The IID Board of Directors not only voted 3–2 against the proposed agreement, but also voted to require the completion of an environmental impact report (EIR) prior to resuming negotiations. The notice of preparation for the EIR stated that IID planned to conserve up to 500,000 acre-feet a year, of which 138,000 acre-feet had already been conserved. The EIR covered potential transfers of up to 250,000 acre-feet a year, and IID estimated the cost of the conservation strategies to be $600 million.

By mid-1986, IID had again broken off negotiations with MWD over the proposed transfer, claiming that MWD was "unwilling to negotiate." At this point, three major stumbling blocks presented themselves. First, IID decided that it would not negotiate for less than $250 per acre-foot, and it also wanted an inflation clause. Second, it wanted a 25-year contract instead of the 35-year contract sought by MWD. Third, IID wanted MWD to agree that it was buying water in exchange for dollars, whereas MWD maintained that it was legally entitled to any conserved water and that IID did not have the right to transfer conserved Colorado River water outside the district's boundaries.

Consistent with their positions, both IID and MWD later prepared draft agreements in November 1987. IID's draft called for an annual payment of $25 million with an escalation clause tied to the Consumer Price Index. Although MWD recognized the need for an operation and maintenance inflation factor, it was unwilling to pay a blanket adjustment. Furthermore, it was only willing to pay $10 million a year or $100 an acre-foot. In addition, IID's draft proposed a 25-year contract term because it believed that in thirty to forty years there would be fewer legal constraints on Colorado River water. MWD, on the other hand, insisted on a 35-year contract as the minimum necessary to plan for future growth in Southern California. Further, IID's draft agreement stated that it would have no obligation to provide MWD with conserved water in any year MWD was already receiving 650,000 acre-feet of Colorado River water. MWD would still be required to pay, however, whether or not it received any conserved water. MWD adamantly opposed this provision. With surplus flows on the Colorado River and water it

---

entered into an agreement whereby Imperial Dam and the All-American Canal were built for the delivery of the district's allotment of Colorado River water. IID, acting as trustee for its water user beneficiaries, charges for this delivery service, which today represents the operation and maintenance costs of the system. IID customers pay around $11 per acre-foot for diversion and transportation of the water.

received as a result of other transfers, it might not receive any IID water in more than half the years of the agreement, but it would be contractually obligated to pay for the water. The quality of the Colorado River water was never an important item of the negotiations, as MWD's bargaining position was dictated by its need to replace the Colorado River water it was losing to the Central Arizona Project.

From the beginning, both parties differed on the legal significance to be given any conserved water. Although both parties' November 1987 draft agreements stipulated that no water rights were to be transferred to MWD, IID also maintained that according to recent state legislation encouraging voluntary water transfers, and specifically Section 1011 of the California Water Code, it could sell any conserved or surplus water outside its boundaries.[13] MWD, on the other hand, argued that it had the legal right to any water not put to beneficial use by IID and refused to concede that it was "buying" the water.

The question of whether the agreement would be characterized as a "sale" of water or as a conservation agreement was hotly contested during the negotiations.[14] Ultimately the final agreement was written as a conservation agreement and not as a sale of water. The parties went on to agree that the money paid to IID would be placed in a conservation fund over which IID would have absolute discretion. MWD agreed to pay mitigation costs resulting from environmental damage due to the loss of water, lost income from hydroelectric power generation, enclosing canals in populated

---

[13] Cal. Water Code §1011(a) states: "When any person entitled to use water under an appropriative right fails to use all or any part of the water because of water conservation efforts, any cessation or reduction in the use of such water shall be deemed equivalent to a reasonable and beneficial use of water to the extent of such cessation or reduction in use." Section 1011(b) states: "Water, or the right to use of water, the use of which has ceased or been reduced as the result of water conservation efforts . . . may be sold, leased, exchanged."

[14] IID's attorney, John Carter, stated that the various draft agreements contemplated IID making a "guarantee" to MWD that a certain amount of water would be conserved and made available. The guarantee would have required IID to obtain Palo Verde's and Coachella's consent not to assert any right to the conserved water. In return, MWD would pay IID a "premium" for the guarantee. However, Carter stated that MWD felt paying a premium was too close to buying the water. It also felt that it would persuade Palo Verde and Coachella to forgo any assertion of rights to the conserved water.

Tim Quinn of MWD stated that MWD never agreed to pay any premium for IID's obtaining Coachella's and Palo Verde's consent to the agreement. Such a premium flies in the face of its legal position that IID has no right to sell any water since all the Colorado River is appropriated. Moreover, MWD did not believe IID should profit from wasting water by receiving a monetary premium.

areas, and litigation. In the executed agreement, MWD agreed to a one-time, up-front payment of $23 million for indirect costs. Although the money is meant to fund various mitigation projects, IID has the flexibility to determine how to use the funds to benefit IID ratepayers.

During the spring of 1988, the draft agreements called for the conservation of 150,000 acre-feet a year, but price continued to prevent resolution of a contract. MWD agreed to annual payments of $15 million, but IID insisted on $17.5 million per year.

On September 7, 1988, the State Water Resources Control Board issued Decision 88–20, which convinced IID that time was running out to conclude a water transfer agreement. Decision 88–20 ordered IID to submit to the board by January 1, 1989, a "specific written plan of implementation containing a definitive schedule" for the conservation of at least 100,000 acre-feet a year by January 1, 1994. Moreover, IID was required to identify the source of funding for the water conservation measures and submit "proof of diligent efforts to secure funding" sufficient to implement the conservation measures. IID was further required to submit semiannual progress reports commencing July 1, 1988, showing the status of the district's water conservation program and, moreover, to have actually achieved conservation of 20,000 acre-feet a year by January 1, 1991.

The importance of Decision 88–20 should not be underestimated. John Carter, IID's attorney, characterized it as introducing an element of uncertainty into any challenge IID might bring. This uncertainty involves the board's authority to declare IID's lack of compliance an unreasonable use of water under Article X, Section 2, of the California Constitution. Carter also said that the confirmation of the board's authority served notice that its jurisdiction was greater than that set out in the Water Code and that as the board evolves and assumes a more expansive role in the state, more pressure will be brought to bear on all water users. If IID was going to be forced to conserve, it might as well, in the process, attempt to get the best and most efficient water delivery system possible. (MWD says that Decision 88–20 pulled the negotiating rug out from under IID.) Eight years had passed since John Elmore first brought allegations of misuse of water against IID, and the board finally appeared willing to live up to its constitutionally mandated responsibility.

After Decision 88–20 was issued, IID hired Bob Edmonton to negotiate a deal with MWD. Because the parties were unable to arrive at a price per acre-foot, they decided to go back to their original plan whereby they would identify specific conservation projects and determine the cost and water conserved on a project-by-project basis. IID had been opposed to this method because it thought it would give MWD too much influence in the Imperial Valley. MWD now claims that the conservation projects to be undertaken were chosen not because they were the cheapest, but rather because they would be best for the system as a whole. MWD estimates that it is paying about $128 per acre-foot annually.[15] When the cost of pumping the water to its customers is added, MWD pays $148 per acre-foot a year.

Both MWD and IID are pleased that an agreement has been worked out, and both are satisfied with the result. IID believes it will have an excellent water delivery system at MWD's expense. MWD, for its part, thinks the negotiation of the contract was worthwhile and says it would do it again. In fact, MWD reports that it is continuing to negotiate for an additional 150,000 acre-feet a year to be conserved, although strategies to conserve additional water would concentrate on farm management techniques and could cost more than $128 per acre-foot annually. (IID, however, flatly denies any ongoing negotiations to transfer additional water.) IID would also like to conserve additional water for local economic growth.

The Agreement

The "Agreement for the Implementation of a Water Conservation Program and Use of Conserved Water" between IID and MWD was executed on December 22, 1988, thus bringing IID into compliance with the January 1, 1989, deadline specified in Decision 88–20. The agreement is divided into sixteen "articles," each composed of various subsections. The term of the agreement extends to December 31 of the year that falls thirty-five years after the completion of the last project of the Conservation Program or the initial operation of that project, whichever is later.

The "Conserved Water Supply" and "Legal Considerations" sections of the agreement state that IID's obligation is to make available to the secretary of the interior conserved water in an amount

---

[15] There apparently are a number of different ways to calculate price per acre-foot. MWD says that it calculates everything in terms of present value. It uses the discount rate as the borrowing rate and determines what bond payments would be to pay all project costs, including capital costs and operation and maintenance costs and amortizes it over a 35-year period. Although this sets the price on the high side, MWD believes it is the most accurate way to determine the price per acre-foot.

equal to the quantity of water conserved by the program. MWD's duty under the agreement is to fund the conservation measures— including the construction and related costs and the ongoing costs necessary to allow IID to conserve water. The program will be administered by a Program Coordinating Committee (PCC) composed of three members: one representative appointed by each of the parties individually plus a third member mutually appointed by them. Section 1.4 requires IID to have all the projects of the program operating within five years of the effective date of the agreement.

The program envisions the construction of "structural and non-structural projects generally consisting of the lining of canals, construction of reservoirs and interceptors, installation of gates and automation equipment together with monitoring and management measures . . . estimated to conserve 100,000 af annually of water for use by MWD." Section 3.2 and Appendix D to the agreement establish a timetable for the implementation of the program's projects and a schedule of water to be conserved:

Effective Date	New Water Conserved and Available for Use by MWD (in acre-feet/year)	Cumulative Amount of New Water Conserved and Available for Use by MWD (in acre-feet/year)
January 1, 1990	38,610	38,610
January 1, 1991	14,745	53,335
January 1, 1992	10,490	63,845
January 1, 1993	22,940	86,785
January 1, 1994	13,215	100,000
January 1, 1995[a]	—	100,000

[a] And each year thereafter until modified pursuant to section 3.3.

As shown in the table, the target deadline for the implementation of the conservation measures is December 1994. Each project will be reviewed yearly for the five years following the effective date of the agreement by consultants who will report their findings to the PCC. If the consultants recommend an adjustment in the estimates of the amount of water being conserved, the PCC will act to adjust those estimates to reflect the actual amount of water being conserved by each project. After the first five yearly reviews, each project will be reviewed once every five years during the balance of the term of the agreement. If it is determined by the PCC, by a court, or by arbitration that more than 100,000 acre-feet a year is being conserved, the excess water will go to MWD. The rationale for MWD getting the excess conserved water is that the agreement is based on a project-by-project formula rather than a price per acre-foot. If the amount of water being conserved is less than 100,000 acre-feet a year, however, IID must undertake additional conservation measures to be funded by MWD.

IID is authorized to prepare project plans and cost estimates for the program's projects to be submitted to the PCC for approval. Barring modification of the proposed plans by the PCC, the Imperial District may then prepare plans and cost estimates for the program's projects to be submitted to the PCC for review and approval. The PCC must approve the final plans before IID can commence bidding procedures. If IID decides to construct any project "with its own forces," it must prepare and submit a schedule of reimbursable costs for PCC approval.

Before nonstructural projects are implemented, the PCC must approve all necessary environmental documentation and reports setting forth the projects' costs. In addition to maintaining the "constructed" program, IID must prepare, before construction is completed, detailed operation and maintenance manuals which will serve as the basis for the annual budget and funding calls defined in the agreement as "ongoing direct annual costs."

MWD must fund not only IID's ongoing direct annual costs of nonstructural projects—which include program operations and maintenance costs—but also the replacement costs of the structural projects necessary for the proper functioning of the program during the term of the agreement. MWD will also fund the capital costs of the program. Moreover, beginning the third year after the effective date of the agreement, MWD will pay IID $200,000 per year to cover IID's increased costs of insurance and liability related to the ongoing direct costs of the nonstructural projects. Finally, MWD must fund indirect costs in the amount of $23 million to cover the costs and potential obligations IID might incur as a result of implementing the program.[16]

---

[16] The indirect costs could potentially include loss of hydroelectric power revenue, mitigation of adverse impacts on agriculture from increased salinity of water, loss of revenue from reduced water deliveries, public information, lateral canal pipelining, modernization of ancillary features of the IID water supply

MWD's right to receive conserved water is not cumulative. If MWD fails to use all the water conserved by the program during any one calendar year, it will not be entitled to more than 100,000 acre-feet of water the next calendar year. But when MWD acts to "bank" the conserved water received from IID by any "valid banking agreement," the water credited to the bank will be deemed received. In any year in which the secretary of the interior cannot deliver the 3.85 million acre-feet of water to the first three priorities of the Seven-Party Agreement, IID may, at its option, be relieved of its duty to provide the conserved water to MWD. Written notice must be given by IID to MWD before January 1 of any year in which it would have the option of not providing MWD the conserved water.

Article IV of the agreement describes the deadlines by which IID must make funding calls and the dates by which MWD must provide payments. Prior to November 15 of each year of the agreement, IID must prepare and submit a budget to be reviewed by the PCC. During the first sixty days of the agreement, MWD must pay IID $18,342,602—the estimated direct costs of the first year of the program. For all subsequent years, IID will issue a funding call to MWD during the first week of January for PCC-approved portions of the budget. MWD must pay the funding call before January 15 of that year. By July 1 following the effective date of the agreement and on July 1 for the subsequent four years, MWD must pay IID $4.6 million to cover indirect program costs. When the total costs of the program, comprising estimated capital costs and estimated annual costs, are reduced below the totals reported in the appendixes to the agreement, and the availability of conserved water is not reduced below 100,000 acre-feet a year, MWD must pay 25 percent of the total money saved to IID, who will apply the funds to the indirect cost account described in Section 4.4. Funds paid to IID by MWD under the terms of the agreement must not be used by IID for negotiation or legal fees incurred trying to resolve disputes with MWD.

Although the parties entered the agreement so that IID's water conservation efforts would be funded by MWD, the parties wanted to preserve their respective contentions to all other Colorado River water as if the agreement did not exist. Thus even though Section

---

system, environmental mitigation and litigation relating to the program's impact on the water level and quality of the Salton Sea and the New and Alamo rivers, and liability related to the program's operation and maintenance to the extent it exceeds insurance obtained by IID.

6.2(b) explicitly states that the agreement is not intended to "limit or restrict the rights held by either party . . . to divert or use Colorado River water," several other subsections under Section 6.2 appear to embody a certain tension between potential future contentions to Colorado River water rights, which might be brought under Article X, Section 2, of the California Constitution and IID's state-perfected right to divert 2.6 million acre-feet a year of Colorado River water.

Section 6.2(d) states that MWD may not assert any right to water conserved by IID based on the fact that MWD funded all the conservation measures.[17] It also states that the "Agreement will not result in any forfeiture, diminution or impairment of any rights of IID in the conserved water." But the section also expressly states that it does not "constitute a waiver" of MWD's claims to conserved water with respect to the parties' contracts with the secretary of interior or under the Seven-Party Agreement.

Section 6.2(e) states that MWD does not own any of IID's water rights or any of the conservation facilities, improvements, projects, or measures installed or operated by IID. Moreover, the water is to retain its third priority status under the Seven-Party Agreement and MWD may not assert that the agreement and the resulting use of conserved water has caused a shift of priority from IID's third position—or the combined first three priorities totaling 3.85 million acre-feet a year—to MWD's fourth and fifth priorities. This subsection should then be contrasted with Section 6.2(g), which states that "nothing in the Agreement shall constitute a waiver of MWD's contention as to the rights of MWD to receive water not put to beneficial consumptive use by the holders of the first three priorities of the California Seven Party Agreement as set forth in both IID's and MWD's water delivery contracts with the Secretary."[18]

---

[17] In this respect, the agreement mirrors Cal. Water Code §1244, which states: "The sale, lease, exchange, or transfer of water or water rights, in itself, shall not constitute evidence of waste or unreasonable use" of water.

[18] Ibid. When asked about the apparent tension embodied in Article VI of the agreement, IID's attorney said that this particular section was the most difficult to write and it took five years for the parties to agree on the language contained in the agreement. Briefly stated, the way Article X is worded represents the parties' attempt to maintain the status quo. The crux of the issue, as seen earlier, is MWD's belief that Section 1011 of the Water Code is not good law. MWD believes it should be entitled to any water IID does not beneficially use. Others at IID believe it is only a matter of time before MWD will challenge the law and make a grab for the water the southern coastal region of the state desperately needs to support the 5 million new residents that DWR predicts will move to the area by the year 2010.

Third-Party Effects

The Coachella Valley Water District filed a lawsuit for declaratory and injunctive relief against MWD on February 1, 1989. Under the terms of the Seven-Party Agreement, 3.85 million acre-feet a year goes to what are known as the "agricultural agencies" and the Yuma Project/Reservation District. In 1934, IID and Coachella, which together hold the third priority right, entered into an agreement of compromise whereby IID was given the superior right within that third priority. Because Coachella holds the most junior priority among the agricultural agencies, it is attempting to protect itself in the event that the full 3.85 million acre-feet allotment is not delivered by the secretary to the first three priorities under the Seven-Party Agreement.[19] Less than full delivery seems more likely now that the Central Arizona Project is finally going on line.

In essence, Coachella argues that IID's use of Colorado River water is limited to potable and irrigation purposes within the boundaries of IID and the Coachella Valley, that IID has no right to transfer water outside its district, that Coachella's right to use water allocated to the first three priorities under the Seven-Party Agreement is superior to MWD's fourth priority, and that the secretary has no authority to deliver third-priority water to MWD. Coachella bases its allegation that the IID/MWD water transfer is unlawful on its reading of the Boulder Canyon Project Act, the federal government's agreements for the delivery of water entered into with IID and Coachella during the early 1930s, and the holding of the Supreme Court in *Arizona v. California.*

Coachella's complaint places both IID and MWD in a precarious position. IID is under order of the board to achieve conservation of 20,000 acre-feet by June 1, 1990. If it intends to comply with Decision 88–20, it must improve its water delivery system immediately. Similarly, MWD needs the consent of Palo Verde and Coachella in order to receive any of IID's conserved water. Although IID is a named party in the suit, as of April 1989 it had not been

---

[19] According to Charles Shreves of IID, this has only happened once in the past twenty-nine years. This leads both him and Lester Bornt to believe that Coachella's suit is merely an effort to blackmail IID for water. Both indicated that if Coachella wanted conserved water, IID would provide it if Coachella funded additional conservation measures.

served.[20] Both John Carter and Tim Quinn feel confident that the Coachella suit will be settled in the near future. (Such a settlement will most likely entail the negotiation of a compromise agreement regarding Coachella's water right.)

Conclusion

Since the opening of negotiations between the parties in April 1984, the ominous "Owens Valley Syndrome" and the concomitant erosion of an agricultural community's economic and social infrastructure loomed in the minds of Imperial Valley farmers. But once IID received a favorable legal opinion to the effect that California law would control the allocation and distribution of Colorado River water once it enters the state, the district was less concerned about the possible effects of a water transfer agreement on its right to any salvaged water. The main issue for IID has always been the protection of its water rights.

Bolstered by Section 1011 of the California Water Code, IID believes it can comply with Decision 88–20 and retain its rights to any conserved water. MWD, on the other hand, argues that Article X, Section 2, of the California Constitution entitles it—as the next priority user—to any water that IID has not put to a reasonable and beneficial use. Therefore, MWD asserts that IID has no right to "sell" conserved water outside the district's boundaries. The conflict between these positions was evident from the beginning of the negotiations when the parties disagreed on the characterization of the contract: Was it a conservation agreement or a sale of water?

The tension between Section 1011 of the California Water Code and Article X, Section 2, of the California Constitution was the most formidable barrier the parties had to overcome—and was probably the underlying reason for the prolonged negotiations.[21] Article X, Section 2, mandates that the

> water resources of the State be put to beneficial use to the fullest extent of which they are capable, and that the waste or

---

[20] If served, IID will argue that under Section 1011 of the Water Code it is entitled to transfer the water it conserves. But IID thinks MWD does not want to be forced to litigate the Section 1011 issue until it can attack it effectively.

[21] Robert Potter, deputy director of the Department of Water Resources, perceptively notes that five years is not unreasonably long—considering the amount of time it takes to plan new water projects and the length of the contract's lifetime.

unreasonable use or unreasonable method of use of water be prevented, and that the conservation of such waters is to be exercised with a view to the reasonable and beneficial use thereof in the interest of the people and for the public welfare.

The broad language of Section 2 has been interpreted as a dynamic, evolving statement of water policy responsive to statewide considerations. The California Supreme Court has held that "a reasonable use of water depends on the circumstances of each case; such an inquiry cannot be resolved *in vacuo* isolated from statewide considerations of transcendent importance. Paramount among these we see the ever increasing need for the conservation of water."[22]

The California legislature is the ultimate arbiter of the public interest and general welfare, and in 1980 it determined that it would be in the best interest of the people of California to encourage the voluntary transfer of water. To this end, the legislature decided that any cessation or reduction in the use of water resulting from the implementation of water conservation measures would be deemed a "reasonable and beneficial use" of water[23] and resolved that water transfers would put the "water resources of the state to beneficial use to the fullest extent of which they are capable."[24]

It is unfortunate that both the State Board and the courts have been unwilling to use their equitable powers to make findings of waste and unreasonable use of water—thereby encouraging efficient use of this valuable resource. But the State Board is a highly political body and the courts are loath to find long-standing practices unreasonable. Moreover, it is unlikely that the board will be able to examine in detail the water use practices of every appropriator. This approach alone would be too time consuming and inefficient from an administrative standpoint. Any findings of waste would almost certainly result in protracted litigation— delaying resolution of the problems for years, costing taxpayers unnecessary expense, and exacerbating the alleged waste of water at issue.[25] Water transfers are seen by the legislature, the state's water bureaucracy, and environmentalists alike as pragmatic

---

[22] *Joslin v. Marin Municipal Water District*, 67 Cal. 2d 132, 141 (1967).

[23] California Water Code §1011.

[24] California Constitution, Art. X, §2.

[25] See Environmental Defense Fund, *Trading Conservation Investments for Water* (March 1983).

means of achieving efficient water use. Nonetheless, as illustrated in this case study, without the board's finding of IID's waste and unreasonable use of water, and without the subtle threats that continued waste could result in the loss of that water, IID and MWD might never have concluded a conservation agreement.

Department of the Interior Water Transfer Policy

Principles Governing Voluntary Water Transactions That Involve or Affect Facilities Owned or Operated by the Department of the Interior

PREAMBLE

Transactions that involve water rights and supplies are occurring pursuant to State law with increasing frequency in the Nation, particularly in the Western United States. Such transactions include direct sale of water rights; lease of water rights; dry-year options on water rights; sale of land with associated water rights;

This policy statement was released by the Department of the Interior in December 1988; the following "Voluntary Water Transactions Criteria and Guidance" text came out in early 1989.

and conservation investments with subsequent assignment of conserved water.

The Federal government, as owner of a significant portion of the Nation's water storage and conveyance facilities, can assist State, Tribal, and local authorities in meeting local or regional water needs by improving or facilitating the improvement of management practices with respect to existing water supplies. Exchanges in types, location or priority of use that are accomplished according to State law can allow water to be used more efficiently to meet changing water demands, and also can protect and enhance the Federal investment in existing facilities. In addition, water exchanges can serve to improve many local and Indian reservation economies.

DOI's interest in voluntary water transactions proposed by others derives from an expectation that, to an increasing degree, DOI will be asked to approve, facilitate, or otherwise accommodate such transactions that involve or affect facilities owned or operated by its agencies. The DOI also wishes to be responsive to the July 7, 1987, resolution of the Western Governors' Association, which was reaffirmed at the Association's July 12, 1988, meeting, that the DOI "develop and issue a policy to facilitate water transfers which involve water and/or facilities provided by the Bureau of Reclamation."

The following principles are intended to afford maximum flexibility to State, Tribal, and local entities to arrive at mutually agreeable solutions to their water resource problems and demands. At the same time, these principles are intended to be clear as to the legal, contractual, and regulatory concerns that DOI must consider in its evaluation of proposed transactions.

For the purpose of this statement of principles, all proposed transactions must be between willing parties to the transaction and must be in accordance with applicable State and Federal law. Presentation of a proposal by one party, seeking Federal support or action against other parties, will not be considered in the absence of substantial support for the proposal among affected non-Federal parties.

Voluntary Water Transaction Principles

1. Primacy in water allocation and management decisions rests principally with the States. Voluntary water transactions under this policy must be in accordance with applicable State and Federal laws.

2. The Department of the Interior (DOI) will become involved in facilitating a proposed voluntary water transaction only when it can be accomplished without diminution of service to those parties otherwise being served by such Federal resources, and when:

(a) there is an existing Federal contractual or other legal obligation associated with the water supply; or

(b) there is an existing water right held by the Federal government that may be affected by the transaction; or

(c) it is proposed to use federally-owned storage or conveyance capacity to facilitate the transaction; or

(d) the proposed transaction will affect Federal project operation; and

(e) the appropriate State, Tribal, or other non-Federal political authorities or subdivisions request DOI's active involvement.

3. DOI will participate in or approve transactions when there are no adverse third-party consequences, or when such third-party consequences will be heard and adjudicated in appropriate State forums, or when such consequences will be mitigated to the satisfaction of the affected parties.

4. As a general rule, DOI's role will be to facilitate transactions that are in accordance with applicable State and Federal law and proposed by others. In doing so, DOI will consider the positions of the affected State, Tribal, and local authorities. DOI will not suggest a specific transaction except when it is part of an Indian water rights settlement, a solution to a water rights controversy, or when it may provide a dependable water supply the provision of which otherwise would involve the expenditures of Federal funds. Such a suggestion would not be carried out without the concurrence of all affected non-Federal parties.

5. The fact that the transaction may involve the use of water supplies developed by Federal water resource projects shall not be considered during evaluation of a proposed transaction.

6. One of DOI's objectives will be to ensure that the Federal government is in an acceptable financial, operational, and contractual position following accomplishment of a transaction under this policy. Unless required explicitly by existing law, contracts, or regulations, DOI will refrain from burdening the transaction with additional costs, fees, or charges, except for those costs actually incurred by DOI in performance of its functions in a particular transaction.

7. DOI will consider, in cooperation with appropriate State, Tribal and local authorities, necessary measures that may be required to mitigate any adverse environmental effects that may arise as a result of the proposed transaction.

Voluntary Water Transactions Criteria and Guidance

To assist in the implementation of the December 16, 1988, principles, the following criteria and guidance are provided. It is anticipated that each specific proposed voluntary water exchange will be unique, and that it should be evaluated on its own merits under the overall guidance of this policy statement.

Principle 1. Primacy in water allocation and management decisions rests principally with the States. Voluntary water transactions under this policy must be in accordance with applicable State and Federal laws.

Criterion: Does the proposed exchange comply with applicable State and Federal laws?

Guidance: Apparent conflicts with State laws or water rights will be reconciled with the appropriate State agency. State laws generally provide procedures for transferring water rights, and should be the primary mechanism for protecting the sellers/lessors of water, as well as third parties.

Proposed transactions that involve a new use not specifically authorized as a Federal project purpose, or that propose a place of use not within the Federal project service area, may require authorizing legislation. The primary responsibility for such legislation will rest with those entities proposing the transaction.

Principle 2. The Department of the Interior (DOI) will become involved in facilitating a proposed voluntary water transaction only when it can be accomplished without diminution of service to those parties otherwise being served by such Federal resources, and when:

1. There is an existing Federal contractual or other legal obligation associated with the water supply; or
2. There is an existing water right held by the Federal Government that may be affected by the transaction; or
3. It is proposed to use federally-owned storage or conveyance capacity to facilitate the transaction; or
4. The proposed transaction will affect Federal project operations; and
5. The appropriate State, Tribal, or other non-Federal political authorities or subdivisions request DOI's active involvement.

Criterion: Does the proposed action involve water that is encumbered by an existing Federal contractual obligation?

Guidance: If revision of existing water service or repayment contracts is required to facilitate an otherwise desirable water exchange proposal, negotiations for those changes will be initiated expeditiously under the guidance of these principles and the appropriate legal authorities pertaining to the subject water.

Criterion: Does the proposed action potentially affect a Federal water right?

Guidance: In those instances where the United States' water rights may be affected by a water transaction, DOI will work to facilitate the transfer so long as its rights or the rights of its contractors are protected or adequately compensated. In the evaluation of a proposed action, effects on existing water rights should be an initial consideration. If the proposed action would appear to involve lengthy and costly legal procedures in either the State or Federal courts, this information should be provided to the proposing parties. The policy does not provide for the avoidance of State and Federal laws and procedures in the establishment of water allocations and water rights.

Criterion: Does the proposed action propose the use of Federal storage/conveyance capacity?

Guidance: Federal facilities may be used to store/transfer both federally and non-federally supplied water. The Warren Act provides the basis for storage/transfer of non-federally supplied water for irrigation. Storage/transfer

171

of non-federally supplied water for municipal and industrial (M&I) purposes can be accomplished generally under the authority of section 9(c) of the Reclamation Project Act of 1939.

Except by mutual consent of affected parties, contracts for additional storage/conveyance will take into account existing Federal contracts, conveyance capacity and project obligations which must be honored as a first priority.

Approval to transfer water cannot obligate the Federal Government to incur extra nonreimbursed expense to store water or to convey it to a new location.

Approval to transfer water will not establish any right to future transfers beyond those expressly provided for in negotiated agreements.

Use of storage/conveyance will require a supporting contract to use federally built storage/conveyance systems.

Charges will be set to recover normally allocable storage, delivery, or extra costs incurred by the U.S.

If any additional pumping power is needed to effect a given transfer, the transfer entities must provide or pay for such power, and may have to secure it from non-Federal sources.

Proposals may involve the Corps of Engineers' facilities or projects. In these cases, consideration of their concerns will be included in the evaluation of the specific proposal.

Criterion: Does the proposed action affect existing Federal project operations?

Guidance: With a change in type, location, or priority of use, the potential for effects on the authorized purposes and project operations must be investigated. For example, such effects could result from changes in operation of a reservoir or delivery system, that might change minimum stream flow or power generation. If these potential effects are identified, avoidance of these consequences, or mitigation of such consequences to the satisfaction of the affected party, is necessary.

As stated in the guidance area 2(b), DOI will work to facilitate the proposed transfer so long as its (water)

172

rights or the (water) rights of its contractors are protected or adequately compensated; and in guidance area 2(c), except by mutual consent of affected parties, contracts for additional storage/conveyance will take into account existing Federal contracts and project obligations.

Power interference charges or similar compensation measures will be the responsibility of those entities proposing the transaction.

In addition to the evaluation of effects on existing project operations, and authorized project beneficiaries, the following general issues must also be addressed:

1. Third-party effects. See Principle 3.
2. Documentation for compliance with NEPA. See Principle 7.
3. Land Classification. If the proposed action is a change in location of use for irrigation water, land classification is necessary to ensure that the land is capable of sustaining irrigation activities without damage to the land or water resource. Demonstration that sufficient payment capacity exists during the term of the transfer may also be required. The level of detail, amount of original work, and depth of analysis will be determined on the merits of each situation.
4. Reclamation Reform Act of 1982. If the existing contract must be changed to allow the proposed exchange, the discretionary provisions of the Reclamation Reform Act of 1982 must be considered. For further guidance on supplemental or additional benefits and the amendments to existing contracts, refer to the Solicitor's memorandum dated May 20, 1988, "Interpretation of Section 203(a) of the Reclamation Reform Act of 1982 and Sections 105 and 106 of Public Law 99-546." Additional guidance is contained in the Acreage Limitation Rules and Regulations on contracts, additional and supplemental benefits, and water transfers.

Criterion: Does the proposed action stem from a request by a State, Tribe, or non-Federal agency?

Guidance: DOI will continue its policy of providing technical assistance to State, Tribal, or local agencies. A positive and expeditious technical assistance/consultation program will continue within available budget resources.

The specific involvement of DOI necessary to accommodate the requested exchange will determine the type of Reclamation involvement. Existing procedures for approving new or amendatory contracts should be followed.

Principle 3. DOI will participate in or approve transactions when there are no adverse third-party consequences, or when such third-party consequences will be heard and adjudicated in appropriate State forums, or when such consequences will be mitigated to the satisfaction of the affected parties.

Criterion: Concerns for third-party effects must be addressed from both the State and the Federal perspective. Any consideration of the "public trust doctrine" is left to the State.

Guidance: Concerns for authorized project functions and operations were addressed in Principle 2. This principle addresses the concerns for "third-party" effects. Third parties are identified as those entities who may have some identifiable interest in the exchange, and would have a legal standing in an adjudication process in an appropriate State forum. The identification of these entities, the validity of their concerns, and the appropriate satisfaction of their concerns rests with the States and their adjudication process.

Principle 4. As a general rule, DOI's role will be to facilitate transactions that are in accordance with applicable State and Federal law and proposed by others. In doing so, DOI will not suggest a specific transaction except when it is part of an Indian water rights settlement, a solution to a water rights controversy, or when it may provide a dependable water supply, the provision of which otherwise would involve the expenditure of Federal funds. Such a suggestion would not be carried out without the concurrence of all affected non-Federal parties.

Criterion: Does the proposed action displace the need for expenditure of Federal funds?

Guidance: Within Reclamation's resource management program, opportunities will be explored to achieve management objectives through the use of voluntary exchanges of water. The intent of this policy is to ensure that voluntary exchanges of water are considered as alternatives in water resource management within Reclamation's planning, operation, and other resource development programs. For example, a water exchange may be considered as an alternative to construction of a storage or delivery facility that otherwise would or could require Federal investment.

Criterion: Does the proposed action provide for an opportunity for the Indian tribe or community to benefit economically from the lease or transfer of water rights that may be secured under a settlement with the Federal Government or with non-Federal parties?

Guidance: It is a common situation that the water rights available to Indian tribes represent a significant portion of their resource base. It also is a common situation that the use of those water resources for agricultural purposes is marginally feasible, and that local water demands by non-Indians are such that the lease or transfer of the tribal water resources can be a mutually beneficial transaction.

DOI will facilitate transfers, in its capacity as a trustee, for an Indian tribe to the extent that it results in assisting local water users in resolving their water resource management problems within appropriate state law. The specific authorities involved will be determined on a case specific evaluation of the water rights, Federal and State laws, and the specific nature of the proposed transaction.

Principle 5. The fact that the transaction may involve the use of water supplies developed by Federal water resource projects shall not be considered during the evaluation of a proposed transaction.

Criterion: Is the water to be transferred, exchanged, leased, sold, etc., available by virtue of a Federal Reclamation project?

175

Guidance: If the Federal Government is not made worse off financially by the transaction, if the proposed transaction has been approved by the State and local authorities, and if the proposed transaction complies with Federal and State law; then it may be in the public interest to allow federally developed water to be employed. The fact that it was developed by virtue of a subsidized Federal project or program should not, in and of itself, be a barrier to the transaction.

On the other hand, DOI should seek the most appropriate source for water to be transferred, exchanged, leased, or sold without regard to presently available supplies from Federal projects.

Principle 6. One of DOI's objectives will be to ensure that the Federal Government is in an acceptable financial, operational, and contractual position following accomplishment of a transaction under this policy. Unless required explicitly by existing law, contracts, or regulations, DOI will refrain from burdening the transaction with additional costs, fees, or charges, except for those costs actually incurred by DOI in performance of its functions in a particular transaction.

Criterion: The financial terms negotiated between entities do not concern DOI.

Repayment subsidies associated with the original type of use of the water are not transferable to a different type of use of the water.

Exchanges cannot result in a reduction in the present worth of the outstanding obligations remaining to be repaid to the Federal Government.

If the proposed exchange would involve the execution of a contract with a "new" entity, that entity must have sufficient legal authority to enter into such a contract and be able to perform all functions required by the contract.

Any additional costs associated with the transfer shall be advanced or repaid in a manner negotiated by the entities involved.

Guidance: A distinction must be made between financial terms between the entities proposing the exchange and Federal repayment considerations associated with the water. Financial terms between the non-Federal entities are extraneous to the repayment considerations discussed herein.

1. The costs or subsidies associated with the *original* use are not transferable to a *different* use of the water.
2. A change in use from irrigation to municipal and industrial purpose would require a change in the repayment of costs to include interest during construction and interest on investment, but only to the extent of the remaining years in the payout period. It is not the intent of this water transfer policy to recover subsidies originally allocated to that block of transferred water during the time it served the irrigation.

   A short-term transfer should recognize the repayment of the appropriate cost, with the repayment interest rate, calculated for the year of the transfer, after which the irrigation rate would be reestablished.

   Any repayment of principal above the level that would have been repaid by the irrigators (i.e., the power assistance amount) should be reflected in a reduction in the amount to be repaid through power assistance.
3. An exchange involving change in location and contracting entities, but not a change in use (i.e., irrigation to irrigation), could involve the continuation of the repayment subsidies.
4. An exchange in which there would be a change in use from reimbursable function (e.g., irrigation to anadromous fishery) will require special negotiations. In lieu of special legislation, specific contractual obligations will be identified to ensure that repayment to the Federal Government after the exchange will be no less than the conditions that existed prior to the exchange.
5. To the maximum extent possible, financial or economic disincentives to the transfer or exchange are to be avoided. The additional costs to the transfer or exchange are to be avoided. The additional costs to

the water users, as discussed in these principles (i.e., NEPA documentation, power interference charges, recalculation of water rates, or incremental pumping costs), are all required by existing law, contracts, or regulations. While these are costs to the water user, they are not the disincentives that are to be avoided.

The disincentives to be avoided can be characterized as charging a percentage of any "profit" that might be envisioned as the difference between appropriate costs and the market value of the water.

Principle 7. DOI will consider, in cooperation with appropriate State, Tribal, and local authorities, necessary measures that may be required to mitigate any adverse environmental effects that may arise as a result of the proposed transaction.

Criterion: Is approval of the transaction subject to NEPA requirements?

Guidance: Documentation for compliance with NEPA could range from a categorical exclusion to an environmental impact statement. The type of documentation required will be a function of the specific action being proposed. Any Federal NEPA compliance costs associated with the transfer shall be advanced or repaid in a manner negotiated by DOI and the entities involved.

Appendix C

Bureau of Reclamation Directory

Commissioner's Office

C. Dale Duvall, Commissioner
18th and C Street, NW
Washington, DC 20240
Telephone: 202/343–4662

Denver Office

Joe D. Hall, Deputy Commissioner
P.O. Box 25007
Denver Federal Center
Denver, CO 80225
Telephone: 303/236–7000

Regional Offices

Pacific Northwest Regional Office
Federal Building, U.S. Courthouse
Box 043
550 Fort Street
Boise, ID 83724
Telephone: 208/334–1938

Mid-Pacific Regional Office
Federal Office Building
2800 Cottage Way
Sacramento, CA 95825
Telephone: 916/978–4919

Lower Colorado Regional Office
P.O. Box 427
Nevada Highway and Park Street
Boulder City, NV 89005
Telephone: 702/293–8419

Upper Colorado Regional Office
P.O. Box 11568
125 South State Street
Salt Lake City, UT 84147
Telephone: 801/524–5403

Great Plains Regional Office
P.O. Box 36900
Federal Office Building
316 North 26th Street
Billings, MT 59107–6900
Telephone: 406/657–6218

Selected Bibliography ▄▄▄

Western History and Western Water History

Athearn, R. G. *High Country Empire*. Lincoln: University of Nebraska Press, 1971.

Bain, J. S., et al. *Northern California's Water Industry*. Baltimore: The Johns Hopkins University Press, 1966.

Brower, D. *David R. Brower—Environmental Activist, Publicist, and Prophet*. Berkeley: Bancroft Library Oral History Program, University of California, 1980.

De Voto, B. *Across the Wide Missouri*. Boston: Houghton Mifflin, 1947.

_____. *The Course of Empire*. Boston: Houghton Mifflin, 1952.

El-Ashry, M., and D. Gibbons. *Troubled Waters: New Policies for Managing Water in the American West*. Washington, D.C.: World Resources Institute, 1986.

Garland, H. *A Son of the Middle Border*. New York: Macmillan, 1917.

Gottlieb, R., and P. Wiley. *Empires in the Sun*. New York: Putnam, 1982.

Hollon, W. E. *The Great American Desert, Then and Now.* New York: Oxford University Press, 1966.

Kahrl, W. *Water and Power.* Berkeley: University of California Press, 1982.

Kahrl, W., ed. *California Water Atlas.* Sacramento: Department of Water Resources, 1978, 1979.

Lilley, W., and L. Gould. "The Western Irrigation Movement 1878–1902: A Reappraisal." In Gene Gressley, ed., *The American West: A Reorientation.* Laramie: University of Wyoming Publications, 1966.

McWilliams, C. *California: The Great Exception.* (2nd ed.) Santa Barbara: Peregrine Smith, 1976.

Reisner, M. *Cadillac Desert.* New York: Viking-Penguin, 1986.

Robinson, M. *Water for the West.* Chicago: Public Works Historical Society, 1979.

Shannon, F. A. *The Farmer's Last Frontier.* New York: Farrar and Rinehart, 1945.

Sibley, G. "The Desert Empire." *Harper's,* October 1977.

Stegner, W. *Beyond the Hundredth Meridian.* Boston: Houghton Mifflin, 1953.

Webb, W. P. *The Great Plains.* New York: Ginn, 1931.

Welsh, F. *How to Create a Water Crisis.* Boulder: Johnson Books, 1985.

Worster, D. *Rivers of Empire.* New York: Pantheon, 1985.

Western Water Law

Books and Reports

Anderson, T., ed. *Water Rights: Scarce Resource Allocation, Bureaucracy, and the Environment.* San Francisco: Pacific Institute for Public Policy Research, 1983.

Driver, B. *Western Water: Tuning the System.* Denver: Western Governors' Association, 1986.

Environmental Defense Fund. *Trading Conservation Investments for Water.* Berkeley: Environmental Defense Fund, 1983.

Folk-Williams, J.; S. Fry; and L. Hilgendorf. *Western Water Flows to the Cities*. Santa Fe: Western Network, 1985.

Frederick, K., ed. *Scarce Water and Institutional Change*. Washington, D.C.: Resources for the Future, 1986.

Saliba, B., and D. Bush. *Water Markets in Theory and Practice*. Boulder: Westview Press, 1987.

Wahl, R. *Promoting Increased Efficiency of Federal Water Use Through Voluntary Water Transfers*. Discussion Paper No. FAP87–02. Washington, D.C.: National Center for Food and Agricultural Policy, 1987.

Wahl, R., and F. Osterhoudt. "Voluntary Transfers of Water in the West." In U.S. Geological Survey, *National Water Summary 1985*.

Western Governors' Association, Water Efficiency Working Group. *Water Efficiency: Opportunities for Action*. Denver: Western Governors' Association, 1987.

Law Review Articles

Driver, B. "The Effect of Reclamation Law on Voluntary Water Transfers." *Rocky Mountain Mineral Law Institute* 33 (1987):26-1.

Dunning, H. "Reflections on the Transfers of Water Rights." *Journal of Contemporary Law* 4 (1977):109.

Getches, D. "Management and Marketing of Indian Water: From Conflict to Pragmatism." *University of Colorado Law Review* 58 (1988):515.

_____. "Water Planning: Untapped Opportunity for the Western States." *Journal of Energy Law and Policy* 9 (1988):1.

_____. "Water Use Efficiency: The Value of Water in the West." *Public Land Law Review* 8 (1987):1.

Gheleta, M. "Water Use Efficiency and Appropriation in Colorado: Salvaging Incentives for Maximum Beneficial Use." *University of Colorado Law Review* 58 (1988):657.

Gould, G. "Water Rights Transfers and Third-Party Effects." *Land and Water Law Review* 23 (1988):1.

Howe, C.; D. Schurmeier; and W. Shaw. "Innovative Approaches to Water Allocation: The Potential for Water Markets." *Water Resources Research* 22 (1986):439.

O'Brien, D. "Water Marketing in California." *Pacific Law Journal* 19 (1988):1165.

Pring, G., and K. Tomb. "License to Waste: Legal Barriers to Conservation and Efficient Use of Water in the West." *Rocky Mountain Mineral Law Institute* 25 (1979):25-1.

Roos-Collins, R. "Voluntary Conveyance of the Right to Receive a Water Supply from the United States Bureau of Reclamation." *Ecology Law Quarterly* 13 (1987):773.

Sax, J. "Selling Reclamation Water Rights: A Case Study in Federal Subsidy Policy." *Michigan Law Review* 64 (1965):13.

Shupe, S. "Waste in Western Water Law: A Blueprint for Change." *Oregon Law Review* 62 (1982):483.

Tarlock, A. "The Changing Meaning of Water Conservation in the West." *Nebraska Law Review* 66 (1987):145.

Willey, Z., and T. Graff. "Federal Water Policy in the United States—An Agenda for Economic and Environmental Reform." *Columbia Journal of Environmental Law* 13 (1988):325.

Index

185

187

About the Authors

MARC REISNER was staff writer for the Natural Resources Defense Council from 1972 to 1979. In 1979 he won an Alicia Patterson Journalism Fellowship to investigate the water situation in the American West. That investigation resulted in *Cadillac Desert*, which was nominated for the National Book Critics' Circle Award. Both *Library Journal* and *Publishers Weekly* called *Cadillac Desert* one of the twelve best nonfiction books published in 1986. A graduate of Earlham College, Reisner lives in San Francisco with his wife, Lawrie Mott, and daughter, Ruth.

SARAH BATES is a graduate of Colorado State University and the University of Colorado School of Law. As research assistant for Professor David Getches, she helped to research and edit a water law textbook, *Water Resources Management*, by Meyers, Tarlock, Corbridge, and Getches. She has worked as law clerk with the Environmental Law Institute in Washington, D.C., and for the National Wildlife Federation's Rocky Mountain Natural Resources Clinic in Boulder, Colorado. Currently, Bates is an attorney with the Sierra Club Legal Defense Fund and lives in San Francisco with her husband, Bill Howe.

Also Available from Island Press

The Challenge of Global Warming
Edited by Dean Edwin Abrahamson
Foreword by Senator Timothy E. Wirth
In cooperation with the Natural Resources Defense Council
1989, 350 pp., tables, graphs, index, bibliography
Cloth: $34.95   ISBN: 0-933280-87-4
Paper: $19.95   ISBN: 0-933280-86-6

Crossroads: Environmental Priorities for the Future
Edited by Peter Borrelli
1988, 352 pp., index
Cloth: $29.95   ISBN: 0-933280-68-8
Paper: $17.95   ISBN: 0-933280-67-X

Deserts on the March
By Paul B. Sears
New Introduction by Gus Speth, President, World Resources Institute
Conservation Classic Edition 1988
256 pp., illustrations
Cloth: $29.95   ISBN: 0-933280-46-7
Paper: $19.95   ISBN: 0-933280-90-4

Down by the River: The Impact of Federal Water Projects and Policies on Biodiversity
By Constance E. Hunt with Verne Huser
In cooperation with the National Wildlife Federation
1988, 256 pp., illustrations, glossary, index, bibliography
Cloth: $34.95   ISBN: 0-933280-48-3
Paper: $22.95   ISBN: 0-933280-47-5

The Forest and the Trees: A Guide to Excellent Forestry
By Gordon Robinson
Introduction by Michael McCloskey
1988, 272 pp., indexes, appendixes, glossary, tables, figures
Cloth: $34.95   ISBN: 0-933280-41-6
Paper: $19.95   ISBN: 0-933280-40-8

Holistic Resource Management
By Allan Savory
Center for Holistic Resource Management
1988, 512 pp., plates, diagrams, references, notes, index
Cloth: $39.95   ISBN: 0-933280-62-9
Paper: $24.95   ISBN: 0-933280-61-0

Reforming the Forest Service
By Randall O'Toole
1988, 250 pp., graphs, tables, notes
Cloth: $34.95   ISBN: 0-933280-49-1
Paper: $19.95   ISBN: 0-933280-45-9

Reopening the Western Frontier
From *High Country News*
1989, 350 pp., illustrations, photographs, maps, index
Cloth: $24.95   ISBN: 1-55963-011-6
Paper: $15.95   ISBN: 1-55963-010-8

Reserved Water Rights Settlement Manual
By Peter W. Sly, Director, Conference of Western Attorney
   Generals
Preface by Jim Jones, Attorney General, State of Idaho
1988, 265 pp., index, appendixes, bibliography
Cloth: $34.95   ISBN: 0-933280-72-6
Paper: $22.95   ISBN: 0-933280-71-8

Rivers at Risk: The Concerned Citizen's Guide to Hydropower
By John D. Echeverria, Pope Barrow, and Richard Roos-Collins
Foreword by Stewart L. Udall
In cooperation with American Rivers
1989, 220 pp., photographs, appendixes, indexes
Cloth: $29.95   ISBN: 0-933280-83-1
Paper: $17.95   ISBN: 0-933280-82-3

Sierra Nevada: A Mountain Journey
By Tim Palmer
1988, 352 pp., illustrations, appendixes, index
Cloth: $31.95   ISBN: 0-933280-54-8
Paper: $14.95   ISBN: 0-933280-53-X

Western Water Made Simple
By the Editors of *High Country News*
1987, 256 pp., illustrations, maps
Paper: $15.95   ISBN: 0-933280-39-4

For a complete catalog of Island Press publications,
please write:

   Island Press
   Box 7
   Covelo, CA 95428